MUHAMMAD ﷺ
the Last Prophet
A model for all time

Sayyed Abul Hasan 'Ali Nadwi

UK ISLAMIC ACADEMY

© UK Islamic Academy, 1993, 1995, 1999, 2003, 2006

ISBN 1 872531 10 5 (PB)

All rights reserved. No part of this publication may be reproduced, stored in a retrieval system, or transmitted in any form or by any means, electronic, mechanical, photocopying, recording or otherwise, without the prior permission of the copyright owner.

General Editor: Iqbal Ahmad Azami

Published by
UK Islamic Academy
PO Box 6645
Leicester LE5 5WT
United Kingdom

Website: www.ukiabooks.com
E-mail: info@ukiabooks.com

British Library Cataloguing in Publication Data

A catalogue record for this book is available from the British Library

Typeset: Arrow Photoset
Cover Design: S. Nakhooda
Illustration: J. Russell

Contents

	page
Foreword	5
Preface	7
The Age of Ignorance	11
Before Prophethood	15
After Prophethood	29
In Madinah	65
The Decisive Battle of Badr	73
The Battle of Uhud	83
The Battle of the Ditch	99
The Expedition Against the Banu Qurayzah	109
The Peace Treaty of Hudaybiyyah	115
Inviting the Kings and Rulers to Islam	123
The Expedition to Khaybar	127
The Expedition to Mu'tah	137
The Conquest of Makkah	141
The Battle of Hunayn	155

The Expedition of Ta'if	159
The Tabuk Expedition	165
The Year of Delegations	171
The Farewell *Hajj*	173
The Death of the Messenger of Allah	179
The Prophet's Character and Qualities	191
Workbook	193
Transliteration Table	205
Glossary	207
Names/Kunyahs/Epithets and Titles	211
Communities, Tribes, Clans and Families	214
Places	215

Foreword

All the Prophets were chosen by Allah to guide mankind to the Divine Path. They faced many difficulties and suffered severe hardships in their efforts to call their erring people to obey and worship the One God, Allah.

This book is the last in a series of stories about these Prophets. It portrays a vivid picture of the life and times of Muhammad, the last Prophet (peace and blessings be upon him). It has been written in a style attractive to young people by the renowned Islamic scholar Maulana Sayyed Abul Hasan 'Ali Nadwi, one of the greatest living authorities on Islam, whose works provide material for the text books used in schools and colleges throughout the Arab and Muslim world.

This translation has been prepared especially for young English-speaking Muslims who wish to benefit from the scholarship usually found in Arabic or Urdu publications. *MUHAMMAD, the Last Prophet* is based on the Holy Qur'an and contemporary accounts of events taking place during that period. It offers an authentic account of the early call to Islam, the impact of which is still reverberating around the world.

It is hoped that the reader will appreciate this opportunity to examine Islam from a historical perspective and to understand why it remains so relevant to life today.

My thanks are due to Sis. Aisha Bewley, Sis. Umm Ayman, my daughters Su'ād, Shifa' and my other children for their help in producing this book. May Allah accept this effort and make it a source of inspiration and guidance for all.

Leicester, England **Iqbal Ahmad Azami**
Rabī' al-Awwal 1414 A.H.
August 1993

Preface

Praise be to Allah, the Lord of the Worlds and peace be upon the exalted Messenger of Allah and the Seal of the Prophets, Muhammad, and upon all his family and Companions and those who follow them with sincerity until the Day of Judgement.

No words can express the praise and gratitude I owe to Allah Almighty or describe my happiness as I write this preface to the last book in the series *Stories of the Prophets*. Allah has prolonged my life and blessed me with success in completing this book devoted to the life of the last Prophet (may Allah bless him and grant him peace).

A period of thirty years lapsed between writing the story of the Prophet Musa (peace and blessings be upon him) and the section which begins with the story of the Prophet Shu'ayb and ends with the story of the Prophet 'Isa ibn Maryam (peace and blessings be upon them). No one can be certain of continued life and it was only through Divine kindness and favour that I was able to write about the life of the Prophet specifically for children. Having dedicated myself to the task of writing this book I managed to finish it in a short time. Then I began a definitive work on the life of the Prophet. This small book formed the basis for the larger book, completed at the beginning of Shawwal, 1396 A.H. produced by Dar ash-Shuruq in Jeddah under the title, *as-Sirah an-Nabawiyyah* and published in Cairo in Rabi' al-Awwal, 1398 A.H. (April 1977 C.E.). It has also been translated into English and published by The Academy of Islamic Research & Publications, Lucknow, India, entitled *Muhammad, Rasulullah*).

I have based my work on a summary of *as-Sirah an-Nabawiyyah* by Ibn Hisham, one of the oldest books on the life of the Prophet still in existence. It has had a great effect on the hearts and souls of generations of believers. I have also relied on ancient *Sirah* sources and the celebrated books of *as-Sihah* in *hadith*. As I did not set out to write an academic treatise I have refrained from constantly specifying my sources. The book has been written for enthusiastic young people, not for university scholarship, so references are confined to texts and variants. My large and comprehensive book on the *Sirah* will meet their needs for theological arguments and contemporary studies.

By the power of Almighty Allah, this present work comes in between the *Sirah* written for adults and the books published for children. It can be studied by adolescents or read by non-academics, in their *madrasahs*, libraries and homes. It will also be useful to non-Muslims and can be translated into other languages. It contains the core and summary of the *Sirah*, the wonders and facts of various events, the background to the Islamic call, and the conquests and victories associated with it. Above all, this book will provide the student with a welcome environment in which he or she will find guidance to last a lifetime. It provides the light to illuminate the pathway, the spiritual weapons needed for defence against secularism and satanic influences and the message to carry into the future.

Finally, I praise Allah for the successful conclusion of this work. I thank Him for His gifts and blessings and I ask Him to accept my efforts. I pray that this book will help the

Muslim youth of today to overcome the thorny thickets which obstruct their path. Allah is the One who guides to the right path whomever He wants.

Abul Hasan Ali Nadwi

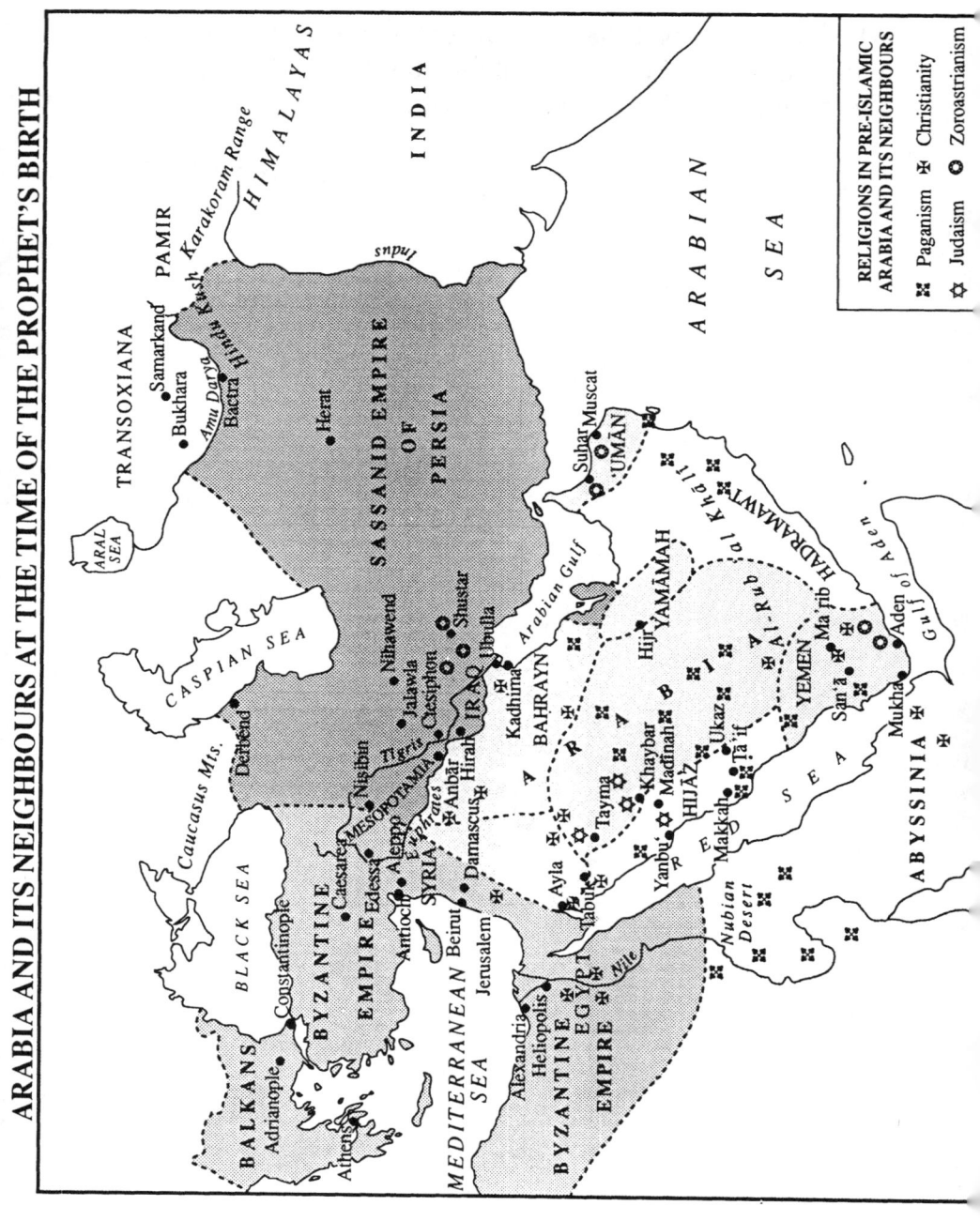

The Age of Ignorance

Ancient religions

After the Prophet of Allah, 'Isa ibn Maryam, there was a long period without a Prophet. Light and knowledge disappeared. Christianity fell into disrepute and became a matter of sport for the corrupt and the hypocrites. From the very beginning, Christianity had been subjected to alterations by extremists and to interpretations by the ignorant. The simple teaching of the Messiah was buried beneath the transgressors' evil behaviour.

The Jews had become a society obsessed with rites and rules lacking all life and spirit. Apart from that, Judaism, a tribal religion, did not carry a message to the world nor a summons to other nations nor mercy to humanity at large.

The Magians were devoted to fire-worship. They built altars and shrines to fire. Outside the shrines they followed their own pursuits. Eventually, no difference whatever could be discerned between the Magians and those with no religion or morality.

Buddhism, a religion widespread in India and Central Asia, was transformed into outright paganism. Altars were built and images of the Buddha set up wherever it went.

Hinduism, the basic religion of India, is distinguished by its millions of idols and gods, and by the unjust separation that exists between its castes, discrimination between the castes being a harsh reality of daily life.

The Arabs also suffered from a paganism and idol-worship of the most abhorrent kind that had no parallel, even in pagan Hindu India. They were involved in *shirk* and adopted gods other than Allah. Every tribe, region or city had a particular idol. Indeed, every house had a private idol. Inside the Ka'bah, the house which Ibrahim (peace be upon him)* had built for the worship of Allah alone, and in its courtyard, stood three hundred and sixty idols.

The Arabian peninsula

The morals of the Arabs were corrupted and they were obsessed with drinking and gambling. Their cruelty and so-called zeal reached the point where they buried baby girls alive. Raiding was widespread as well as highway robbery against trading caravans. The position of women in society was so low that they could be inherited like property or animals. Children were murdered because their parents feared the poverty that would come from raising them.

The Arabs were fond of war and did not hesitate to shed blood. A minor incident could stir up a war lasting for many years in which thousands of people would lose their lives.

---

*Muslims are required to invoke Allah's blessings and peace upon the Prophets whenever their name is mentioned.

Corruption

In short, at this time, mankind was on a suicidal course. Man had forgotten his Creator and was oblivious of himself, his future, and his destiny. He had lost the ability to distinguish between good and evil, and what is beautiful and what is ugly. Throughout vast regions no one was concerned with religion at all and no one worshipped his Lord without associating something with Him. Allah Almighty spoke the truth when He said: *'Corruption has appeared in the land and sea through what the hands of people have earned, that He may let them taste some part of that which they have done, that perhaps they will return.'* (30: 41)

The Prophet is sent to the Arabian peninsula

Allah chose the Arabs to receive the call of Islam and to convey it to the furthest corners of the world. These people were simple-hearted with no complicated ideologies which would have been difficult to remove. While the Greeks, Persians and people of India were arrogant about their many sciences, their fine literature and their splendid civilization, the Arabs followed only simple traditions related to their desert existence. It was not difficult to sweep these away and replace them with a fresh vision.

The Arabs were in a natural state. When it was difficult for them to grasp the truth, they fought it. However, when the covering was removed from their eyes, they welcomed the new beginning and, having embraced it, would risk their lives for it. They were honest and trustworthy, hardy, courageous and fine horsemen. They also possessed a will of iron.

In Makkah, a city in the Arabian peninsula, was the Ka'bah which had been built by Ibrahim and Isma'il (peace be upon them). In it, Allah alone was to be worshipped and it was to be a centre for calling people to *tawhid* for all time. *Tawhid,* meaning the Oneness of Allah, is in sharp contrast with the worship of idols.

> *The first house established for people was that at Bakkah, a blessed place and a guidance for the worlds.* (3: 97)

Before Prophethood

Makkah and the Quraysh

After a long journey, Ibrahim approached Makkah, which lies in a valley between desolate mountains. As there was no water, crops could not grow and human life could not be sustained there. Accompanied by his wife Hajar and his son Isma'il, Ibrahim was fleeing from the cult of idol-worship which had spread throughout the world. He wanted to establish a centre in which Allah alone would be worshipped and to which people could be called. It would be a beacon of guidance and a sanctuary of peace, radiating true faith and righteousness.

Allah accepted Ibrahim's intention and blessed the spot. After Ibrahim had left the inhospitable territory, water flowed from a spring to provide his small family with the means to survive. Hajar and Isma'il dwelt in this arid place far away from other people. Allah blessed the spring of Zamzam and, to this day, people continue to drink its water and to take it with them to all corners of the globe.

While Isma'il was growing up, Ibrahim visited his family. He wanted to sacrifice Isma'il, who was still only a child, in order to show that his love of Allah was greater than his love for his son, just as Allah had commanded him to in a dream. Isma'il also agreed to Allah's command that he should be sacrificed. But Allah saved him and provided a ram from Paradise as a ransom to be sacrificed instead. Isma'il's survival meant that he would be able to help his father in calling people to Allah and to become the ancestor of the last Prophet of Allah, His exalted Messenger.

On a later visit to Makkah, Ibrahim and his son together constructed the Ka'bah, the House of Allah. They prayed to Allah to accept the House and to bless their action. They also beseeched Allah to allow them to live and die in Islam and for Islam to continue after their death. They asked Allah to send a Prophet from among their descendants to renew the call of his ancestor Ibrahim and to complete what he had begun.

'When Ibrahim and Isma'il raised the foundations of the House, praying, "Our Lord, accept this from us. You are the Hearing, the Knowing. Our Lord, and make us surrender to You, and make of our descendants a nation that surrenders to You. Show us our rites and turn to us, You are the One who turns, the Compassionate. Our Lord, and send among them a Messenger from among them who will recite to them Your signs and teach them the Book and the Wisdom and purify them. You are the Mighty, the Wise."' (2: 126–9)

Allah blessed their descendants and the family multiplied in that barren valley. 'Adnan, a descendant of Isma'il (peace be upon him) had many children. Among 'Adnan's descendants Fihr ibn Malik, in particular, was a distinguished chief of the tribe. From Fihr's descendants Qusayy ibn Kilab emerged. He ruled Makkah and held the keys to the Ka'bah. He inspired obedience, was the guardian of the waters of Zamzam and was responsible for feeding the pilgrims. He also presided at the assemblies where the nobles of Makkah gathered for consultation and he held the banner for war. He alone controlled the affairs of Makkah.

Among his sons 'Abd Manaf was the most illustrious, while his eldest son, Hashim became a great man of the people. He provided food and water for the pilgrims coming to Makkah. He was the father of 'Abdu'l-Muttalib, the Messenger of Allah's grandfather, who was also in charge of feeding and giving water to the pilgrims. He was honoured and held in high esteem by his people and his popularity outstripped that of his ancestors. His people loved him.

The descendants of Fihr ibn Malik were called Quraysh. This name came to predominate over all others and the tribe adopted it. All the Arabs recognized the excellent lineage and nobility of the Quraysh. Their eloquence, civility, gallantry and highmindedness were unanimously accepted.

Idol-worship in Makkah

The Quraysh continued to hold to the religion of Ibrahim and Isma'il, glorifying the creed of *tawhid* and the worship of Allah alone, until 'Amr ibn Luhayy became their chief. He was the first to deviate from the religion of Isma'il and to set up idols which he encouraged people to worship. Once he had travelled from Makkah to Syria on business where he saw people worshipping idols. He was so impressed that he brought some idols back to Makkah and set them up, commanding the people there to venerate them.

Traditionally some people would take a few stones from the *Haram,* the sanctuary, with them when they travelled from Makkah as a token of respect for the holy spot. This led to the day when they began to worship any stones they liked. Later generations lost track of the reasons why stones were originally venerated and the Quraysh were happy to worship stone idols just like the people were doing in surrounding countries.

The event of the elephant

During this period a significant event took place which portended another happening of even greater importance. It meant that Allah desired a better future for the Arabs and that the Ka'bah would take on an importance never before attained by any place of worship anywhere in the world.

Abrahah al-Ashram, the viceroy of Negus, the King of Abyssinia, who ruled over the Yemen, built an imposing cathedral in San'a' and named it 'al-Qullays'. He intended to divert the Arab pilgrimage to San'a'. As a Christian, he was jealous that the Ka'bah should be the place where pilgrims gathered and he wanted this position for his church.

The Arabs were stunned by the news. They could not equate any other place with the love and respect they had for the Ka'bah. They could not contemplate exchanging it for any other house of worship. They were preoccupied with the news and discussed it endlessly. An Arab daredevil from the Kinanah tribe went so far as to enter the cathedral and defecate in it. Abrahah was furious when he heard about it and swore that he would not rest until he had destroyed the Ka'bah.

He set out for Makkah with a strong force that included elephants. The Arabs had heard some frightening stories about elephants. They were both distressed and alarmed. Although they wanted to obstruct the progress of

Abrahah's army, they realized that they lacked the power to fight him. They could only leave the matter to Allah and trust to the fact that He was the Lord of the Ka'bah and would protect it. This trust is amply demonstrated by a conversation between Abrahah and the leader of the Quraysh, 'Abdu'l-Muttalib, the grandfather of the Prophet. Abrahah had seized two hundred camels of his, so 'Abdu'l-Muttalib sought permission to see him. Abrahah treated him with respect, descended from his throne and sat down beside him. When Abrahah asked what he wanted, 'Abdu'l-Muttalib replied, 'I want you to return my two hundred camels.'

Abrahah was taken by surprise. He asked, 'Do you wish to speak to me about your two hundred camels that I have taken but say nothing about the House on which your religion and that of your forefathers depends? I have come to destroy it, yet you do not speak to me about it!'

'Abdu'l-Muttalib replied, 'I am the owner of the camels. The House also has an Owner. He will defend it.'

'It will not be defended against me,' retorted Abrahah.

'That remains to be seen,' said 'Abdu'l-Muttalib.

As Abrahah's force drew near, the Quraysh hid high up in the mountains and down in the ravines. They feared the army's approach and waited to see how Allah would save the sacred sanctuary. 'Abdu'l-Muttalib stood with a group of Quraysh and took hold of the door of the Ka'bah, imploring Allah to help them against Abrahah and his army.

Abrahah drew up his soldiers to enter Makkah fully intending to destroy the House. His elephant, whose name was Mahmud, was prepared for the attack. However, the elephant knelt down on the road and refused to get up in spite of severe beatings. When they turned it to face Yemen it got up immediately and moved off.

Allah then sent flocks of birds from the sea; each bird carried stones in its claws. Whenever a stone struck one of Abrahah's soldiers it killed him. The Abyssinians fled in terror, rushing back as the stones hit them. Abrahah was badly hurt. When his soldiers tried to take him with them, his limbs fell off one by one. They took him to San'a' where he died a miserable death.

The Qur'an relates:

'Have you not seen what your Lord did with the people of the Elephant? Did He not make their plan come to nothing. He sent birds against them in flocks, stoning them with stones of baked clay. He made them like eaten stubble.' (105: 1–5)

When Allah repelled the Abyssinians from Makkah, the Arabs' respect for the Quraysh increased. They said, 'These are the people of Allah. Allah fought on their side and helped them to defeat their enemy.'

The Arabs attached great importance to this event and rightly so. They dated their calendar from it, saying, 'This occurred in the Year of the Elephant,' and 'So-and-so was born in the Year of the Elephant' or 'This occurred so many years after the Year of the Elephant.' The Year of the Elephant was 570 in the Christian calendar.

'Abdullah and Aminah

'Abdu'l-Muttalib, chief of the Quraysh, had ten sons. 'Abdullah, the tenth, was the noblest and his father married him to Aminah, daughter of Wahb, leader of the Banu Zuhrah. At that time, her lineage and position made her the best woman in the Quraysh.

However before long 'Abdullah died, leaving a pregnant wife who was to become the mother of the Messenger of Allah. Aminah saw many signs and indications that her son would become an important figure in the future.

Noble birth and pure lineage

The Messenger of Allah (may Allah bless him and grant him peace) was born on Monday, 12 Rabi' al-Awwal, in the Year of the Elephant (570 C.E.). It was the happiest day ever. His ancestry can be traced back to the Prophet Ibrahim (peace be upon him).

His full name is Muhammad ibn 'Abdullah ibn 'Abdu'l-Muttalib ibn Hashim ibn 'Abd Manaf ibn Qusayy ibn Kilab ibn Murrah ibn Ka'b ibn Lu'ayy ibn Ghalib ibn Fihr ibn Malik ibn an-Nadr ibn Kinanah ibn Khuzaymah ibn Mudrikah ibn Ilyas ibn Mudar ibn Nizar ibn Ma'add ibn 'Adnan. The lineage of 'Adnan goes back to the Prophet Isma'il, the son of the Prophet Ibrahim (peace be upon both of them).

The Prophet's mother sent a message to his grandfather, 'Abdu'l-Muttalib, telling him that she had given birth to a boy. He came and looked at the baby lovingly. Then he picked him up and took him into the Ka'bah. He praised Allah and prayed for his grandson whom he named Muhammad. The Arabs were not familiar with this name and were surprised by it.

Babyhood

It was the custom in Makkah for suckling babies to be put in the care of a desert tribe where they grew up in the traditional healthy outdoor environment. 'Abdu'l-Muttalib looked for a wet-nurse for his fatherless grandson, whom he loved more than all his children. Halimah as-Sa'diyah, who received this good fortune had left her home to find a suckling child. It was a year of severe drought and her people were suffering hardship. They needed some income. The baby (may Allah bless him and grant him peace) had been offered to many nurses but they had refused him, because they were hoping for a good payment from the child's father. 'An orphan!' they would exclaim, 'What can his mother or grandfather do?'

Halimah also left him at first but her heart had warmed to him. Allah inspired her with love for this baby so she returned to fetch him and took him home with her. Up until this time she had been an unlucky person but now she found countless blessings. Her animals' udders and her own breasts overflowed with milk and her aged camel and lame donkey were rejuvenated. Everyone said, 'Halimah, you have taken a blessed child.' Her friends envied her.

She continued to enjoy prosperity from Allah until the baby had spent two years with the Banu Sa'd and was weaned. He was growing up differently from the other children. Halimah took him to his mother and asked if she could keep him for a longer period and Aminah agreed.

While the infant, who was to become the Messenger of Allah, was with the Banu Sa'd two angels came and split open his chest. They removed a black clot from his heart and threw it away. Then they cleansed his heart and replaced it.

He tended sheep with his foster brothers and was reared in an uncomplicated, natural environment. He lived the healthy life of the desert and spoke the pure Arabic for which the Banu Sa'd ibn Bakr were famous. He was sociable and popular. His foster brothers loved him and he loved them.

Eventually he returned to Makkah to live with his mother and grandfather. He thrived under Allah's care and grew up to be healthy and strong.

The deaths of Aminah and 'Abdu'l-Muttalib

When the Messenger of Allah was six years old, his mother, Aminah, died. She had taken him to Yathrib to visit her relatives and on the journey back her death occurred at al-Abwa' between Makkah and Madinah. Muhammad (peace and blessings be upon him) must have felt very lonely at this time but he went to stay with his grandfather who was extremely kind to him. He would sit Muhammad (peace and blessings be upon him) on his favourite seat in the shade of the Ka'bah and affectionately caress him.

When the Messenger of Allah (may Allah bless him and grant him peace) was eight, 'Abdu'l-Muttalib also died.

His uncle, Abu Talib

The Messenger of Allah then went to live with his uncle, Abu Talib, the full brother of his father, 'Abdullah. 'Abdu'l-Muttalib had told Abu Talib to take good care of the boy so he was always protective towards him. He treated him with more kindness than he showed to his own sons, 'Ali, Ja'far and 'Aqil.

Divine training

As he grew up, the Messenger of Allah was protected by Allah Almighty. He distanced himself from the obscenities and bad habits of the *Jahiliyyah*. He outshone everyone in manliness, character, modesty, truthfulness, and trustworthiness. He earned respect and the name 'trustworthy'. He respected family ties and shared the burdens of others. He honoured his guests and demonstrated piety and fear of God. He always provided his own food and was content with simple meals.

When he was about fourteen years old, the Fijar War broke out between the tribes of Quraysh and Qays. The Messenger of Allah was at some of the battles, passing arrows for his uncles to fire. He learned about war and about horsemanship and chivalry during these tribal encounters.

Marriage to Khadijah

When the Messenger of Allah was twenty-five, he married Khadijah bint Khuwaylid, a Qurayshi woman of excellent character who was then forty years of age. She had a fine intellect, noble character and great wealth. She had been widowed when her husband, Abu Halah, died.

Khadijah was a businesswoman who hired men to trade goods for her and gave them a share of her profits. The Quraysh were a merchant people. She tested the truthfulness of the Messenger of Allah, his noble character and his sincerity when he took some of her goods to Syria to trade. When she was told about his outstanding competence on this journey she expressed her desire to marry him although she had refused the offer of many noblemen of the Quraysh. The Messenger of Allah also wished to marry her. His uncle Hamzah conveyed the *khitbah,* the marriage proposal, to Khadijah's family and they all readily agreed to it. When the marriage took place Abu Talib delivered the *khutbah* at the ceremony.

Khadijah was the first woman that the Messenger of Allah married and she bore him all his children except Ibrahim.

Rebuilding the Ka'bah

When the Messenger of Allah was thirty-five, the Quraysh decided to rebuild the Ka'bah. Apart from needing a new roof, they found that the stone walls, that were higher than a man's head, had no clay to bind the stones together. They had no alternative but to demolish the building and erect it again.

When the rebuilding had reached the point where the traditional Black Stone had to be put in place, they began to argue. Each clan wanted to have the honour of carrying out this prestigious task. They began to argue fiercely among themselves. During these pagan days far more trivial issues than this could spark off a war.

They prepared to fight. The Banu 'Abdu'd-Dar brought a large bowl filled with blood. They and the Banu 'Adi put their hands in the blood and took a vow to fight to the death.

It was a sign of death and evil. The Quraysh remained in that sorry state for several days, before agreeing that the first person to enter the door of the mosque should make the decision about placing the Black Stone. The first to enter was the Messenger of Allah (may Allah bless him and grant him peace). When they saw him, they said, 'This is the trustworthy one. We are pleased. This is Muhammad.'

The Messenger of Allah called for a piece of cloth. He took the stone and placed it in the centre of the cloth. Then he said that each clan should take a corner of the cloth and lift it together. They did this, bringing it to its position. He put the Black Stone in place with his own hands, and then the building continued.

This was how the Messenger of Allah prevented a war from breaking out among the Quraysh by a supreme demonstration of wisdom.

Hilf al-Fudul

The Messenger of Allah was present at the *Hilf al-Fudul*. This was the most renowned alliance ever heard of in Arabia. It was formed because a man from Zabid had arrived in Makkah with some merchandise and al-'As ibn Wa'il, one of the Quraysh nobles, bought goods from him and then withheld payment. The Zabidi asked the Quraysh nobles for help against al-'As ibn Wa'il, but they refused to intervene because of his position. The Zabidi then appealed to the people of Makkah as a whole for support.

All the fair-minded young men were full of enthusiasm to put the matter right. They met in the house of 'Abdullah ibn Jud'an who prepared food for them. They made a covenant by Allah that they would unite with the wronged man against the one who had wronged him until the matter was settled. The Arabs called that pact *Hilf al-Fudul*, 'The Alliance of Excellence'. They said, 'These people have entered into a state of excellence.' Then they went to al-'As ibn Wa'il and took from him what he owed to the Zabidi and handed it over.

The Messenger of Allah was proud of this alliance. He held it in such high esteem that, after receiving the message of Islam, he said, 'In the house of 'Abdullah ibn Jud'an, I was present at an alliance which was such that if I was invited to take part in it now in Islam, I would still do so.' The Quraysh pledged to restore to everyone what was their due and not to allow any aggressor to get the better of those he had wronged.

In Allah's wisdom, His Messenger was allowed to grow up unlettered. He could neither read nor write. Thus, he could never be accused by his enemies of altering other ideologies. The Qur'an indicates this when it says, *'Before this you did not recite any Book nor write it with your right hand, for then those who follow falsehood would have doubted.'* (29: 48)

The Qur'an called him 'unlettered' and said, *'those who follow the Messenger, the Unlettered Prophet, whom they find written down with them in the Torah and Evangel.'* (7: 157)

MAKKAH MUKARRAMAH

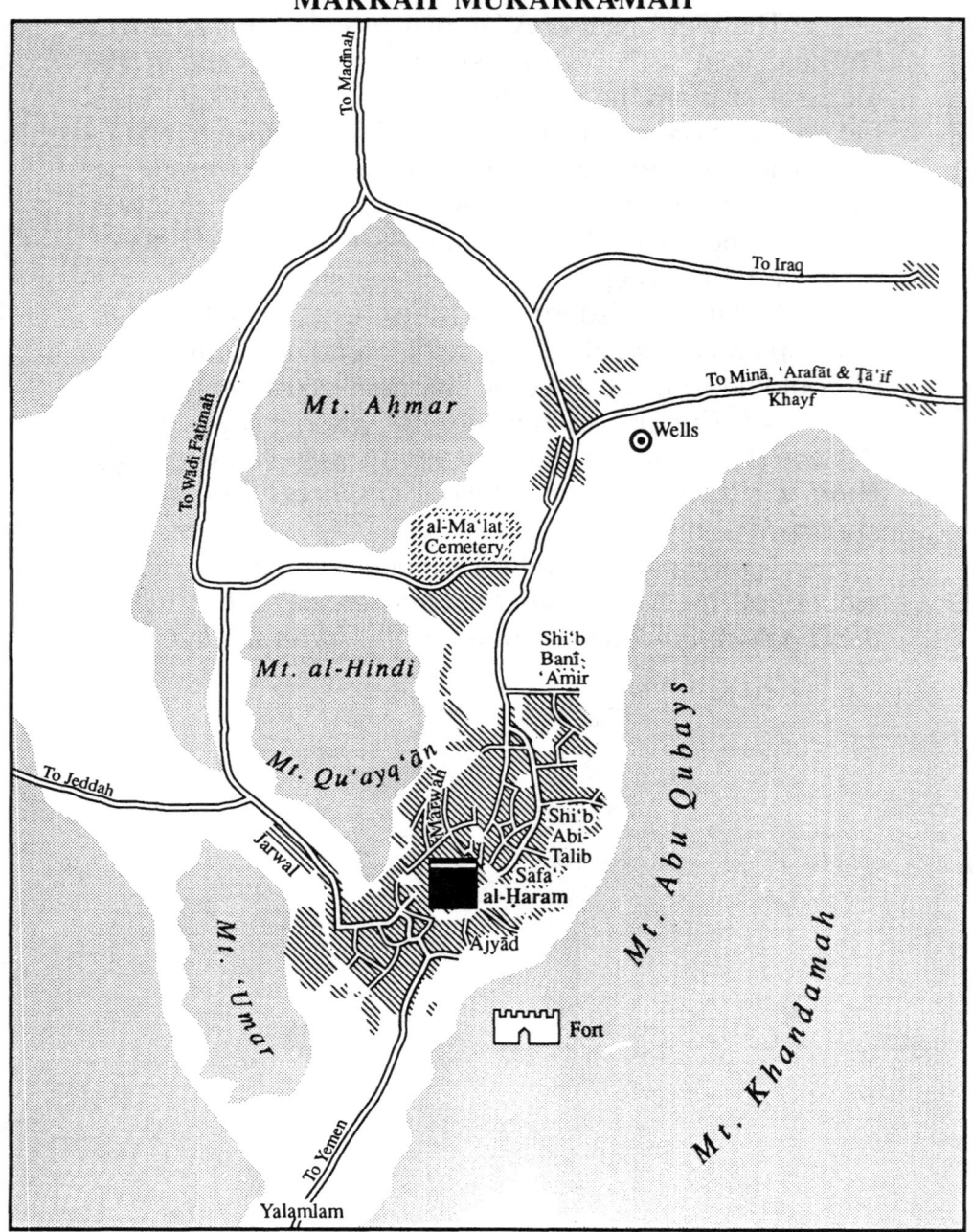

After Prophethood

Intimations of Prophethood

The Messenger of Allah (may Allah bless him and grant him peace) was forty when the first glimpses of light and of his future happiness appeared. The time of his mission approached. It had always been the Divine practice that whenever the darkness had become too intense and the wickedness widespread, a Messenger appeared.

The Messenger of Allah's distaste for what he saw reached a peak. It was as if he was being guided towards a certain spiritual destination. He loved going into retreat. He was always content when he could be on his own. He used to walk away from Makkah until he was well out of sight of the houses. He got to know all the paths, the flat areas and the valleys outside Makkah. From every rock or tree he passed he heard, 'Peace be upon you, Messenger of Allah.' But when he looked around, to his right, to his left and behind him, he could see nothing but trees and rocks.

The first intimations of the future came in the form of dreams, so vivid that they were as clear as the break of day.

The Cave of Hira'

The Messenger of Allah usually went to the Cave of Hira'. He would remain there for several nights in a row, having taken along with him enough food to last for that time. He used to worship and pray in the manner of his ancestor, Ibrahim, the *hanifiyyah*, and followed the pure human need to turn to Allah.

The mission begins

The Messenger of Allah was alone in the Cave of Hira' on the day destined for the start of his prophetic mission. He was forty-one years old and it was the seventeenth day of Ramadan, the sixth of August 610 C.E.

Suddenly an angel appeared and said to him, 'Read!'

'I cannot read,' he replied.

Later, the Messenger of Allah, when recounting what had happened, said, 'He seized me and squeezed me as hard as I could bear and then let me go and said, "Read!"

'I said, "I cannot read."

'Then he squeezed me as hard as I could bear a second time and let me go. Again he said, "Read."

'I cannot read.'

'Then he squeezed me a third time and let me go and said:

"Read in the name of your Lord Who created, created man of a blood-clot. Read, and your Lord is the Most Generous, Who taught by the Pen, taught man what he did not know." ' (96: 1–5)

This was the first day of his prophethood and these were the first verses of the Qur'an to be revealed.

Khadijah's reaction

Naturally, the Messenger of Allah was alarmed by

the experience. He had not known what was happening and he had not heard of anything like this ever happening before. It had been a long time since there had been a Prophet. In any case, the Arabs had only a remote connection with prophethood. He was very frightened and returned to his house trembling.

'Wrap me up! Wrap me up!' he said. 'I fear for myself!'

When Khadijah asked why, he told her what had happened. She was an intelligent lady and had heard of prophethood, Prophets and angels. She used to visit her cousin, Waraqah ibn Nawfal, who had become a Christian. He had read many books and had learned much from the people of the Torah and the Evangel.

Khadijah knew the character of the Messenger of Allah better than anyone because she was his wife and close to his thoughts. She was well aware of his noble character and enviable qualities. She realized that he had always been given success and support by Allah, he was a man chosen from among His creation, whose life and conduct He was pleased with.

No one with a character like his need ever be in fear of Satan or of being affected by the *jinn*. That would be incompatible with what Khadijah knew of the wisdom and compassion of Allah and His way of dealing with His creation. She declared with trust and belief, strongly and forcefully,

'No! Allah would never disgrace you! You maintain close ties with your relations, you bear others' burdens and give people what they need. You are hospitable to your guests and help those with a just claim to get what is due to them.'

Waraqah ibn Nawfal

Khadijah thought it would be a good idea to consult her cousin, the scholar Waraqah ibn Nawfal, and she took the Messenger of Allah to see him. When Waraqah heard what he had seen, he said, 'By the One who holds my soul in His hand, you are the Prophet of this people. The same Great Spirit has come to you which came to Musa. Your people will reject you, abuse you and drive you out and fight you.'

The Messenger of Allah was astonished at what Waraqah said, especially about the Quraysh driving him out because he knew his position among them. They had always addressed him as the 'truthful' one and the 'trustworthy' one.

In amazement he asked, 'Will the people drive me out?'

'Yes,' Waraqah said, 'No man has ever brought anything like what you have brought without his people opposing him and fighting him. If I am alive on that day, and I have already lived a long time, I will give you strong support.'

After this first revelation there was a long gap before the revelations began again. Then the Qur'an started to come down at regular intervals over the following twenty-three years.

Khadijah's Islam and her character

Khadijah hated the behaviour of the people of Makkah, as anyone of sound mind would have detested the atrocities committed by them. She was the first to believe in Allah and His Messenger. She was always at her husband's side helping him through difficult times. She used to lighten his burden and offer him comfort while assuring him of her confidence in his Message.

'Ali ibn Abi Talib and Zayd ibn Harithah accept Islam

After Khadijah, 'Ali ibn Abi Talib (may Allah be pleased with him) accepted Islam. He was ten years old at the time and living in the house of the Messenger of Allah. When Abu Talib went through a period of hardship during a famine, the Messenger of Allah had taken his son 'Ali into his own home and brought him up.

Zayd ibn Harithah, the freed slave of the Messenger of Allah, whom he had adopted, also became a Muslim. The Islam of these people reflected the beliefs of those who knew the Messenger of Allah best. They had witnessed his truthfulness, sincerity and good behaviour. The people who live in a house always know best what is in it.

Abu Bakr ibn Abi Quhafah accepts Islam

Abu Bakr ibn Abi Quhafah also accepted Islam. He had a high position among the Quraysh because of his intellect, strength and sense of justice. He made his Islam known. He was a simple, likeable man who knew the full history of the Quraysh. He was a merchant known for his good character and fair dealing. He began to call others to Allah and those of his friends whom he trusted would come and sit with him to discuss the new ideas.

Quraysh noblemen accept Islam

Through Abu Bakr's work, some of the powerful Quraysh noblemen became Muslims. 'Uthman ibn 'Affan,

Zubayr ibn al-'Awwam, 'Abdu'r-Rahman ibn 'Awf, Sa'd ibn Abi Waqqas and Talhah ibn 'Ubaydullah were among those he brought to the Messenger of Allah.

They were followed by other influential men of the Quraysh, including Abu 'Ubaydah ibn al-Jarrah, al-Arqam ibn Abi'l-Arqam, 'Uthman ibn Maz'un, 'Ubaydah ibn al-Harith ibn al-Muttalib, Sa'id ibn Zayd, Khabbab ibn al-Aratt, 'Abdullah ibn Mas'ud, 'Ammar ibn Yasir, and Suhayb (may Allah be pleased with them all).

Men and women flowed into Islam until everyone in Makkah was talking about the new faith.

The call to Islam on Mount Safa

The Messenger of Allah kept his mission secret for three years. Then Allah commanded him to display His religion openly, saying, *'Loudly proclaim what you are commanded and turn away from the idolworshippers.'* (15: 94) He also said, *'Warn your clan, your nearest kin, and lower your wing to those of the believers who follow you'* (26: 214–15) and *'Say: I am the clear warner.'* (15: 89)

The Prophet climbed up on to the mountain of Safa and called out as loudly as he could, *'Ya Sabahah!'*

This was a well-known cry used to assemble the community in an emergency. When there was any danger of an enemy attacking a city or a tribe, the call, *'Ya Sabahah!'* would ring out. The Quraysh were always quick to respond. They gathered round the Messenger of Allah, who said, 'O Banu 'Abdu'l-Muttalib! O Banu Fihr! O Banu Ka'b! If I told you that there were horses on the other side of this mountain about to attack you, would you believe me?'

The Arabs were practical and realistic. They saw in front of them a man noted for his truthfulness, trustworthiness and sincerity standing on a mountain. He was able to see both what was in front of him and behind him, while they could only see what was in front of them. Their intelligence and sense of justice allowed them to confirm this statement.

'Yes,' they replied.

Then the Messenger of Allah said, 'I warn you of a terrible punishment.'

The people were silent, except Abu Lahab who said, 'May you perish for this! Did you only summon us here for this?'

Enmity of the Quraysh and Abu Talib's concern

When the Messenger of Allah openly proclaimed the call to Islam and called out the truth as he had been commanded to do by Allah, his people did not distance themselves from him nor reject him. However, when he criticized their gods, they regarded him as a menace and united in opposition against him.

His uncle, Abu Talib, concerned about the Messenger of Allah, protected him and stood up for him. The Prophet continued in his mission, loudly proclaiming the truth. Nothing deterred him and Abu Talib continued to care for him and defend him.

Eventually, a group of men of the Quraysh went to Abu Talib threatening, 'Abu Talib! Your nephew has cursed our gods and criticized our religion and ridiculed our customs and called our fathers misguided. Either leave him to us or there will be a split between us and you. You have the same religion and creed as we do.'

Abu Talib spoke reassuringly to them, and they left satisfied. However, the Quraysh constantly discussed the

Messenger of Allah and goaded each other on. They went to Abu Talib a second time, saying, 'Abu Talib! You have age, honour and position among us. We had hoped that you would stop your nephew, but you have not done so. By Allah, we cannot endure any longer this cursing of our fathers and ridiculing of our customs and criticism of our idols. Let us have him or we will put him and you in such a position that one or other of us will be destroyed.'

The division and enmity of his people was a terrible burden for Abu Talib but he did not want to surrender the Messenger of Allah to them. He said, 'Nephew, your people have come to me with threats. Spare me and yourself and do not burden me with more than I can bear.'

'If the sun had been placed in my right hand and the moon in my left . . . '

The Messenger of Allah saw that Abu Talib was very upset by what had happened and was finding it hard to carry on helping him. He said, 'Uncle, by Allah, if they were to place the sun in my right hand and the moon in my left hand on condition that I abandon this business, I would still not leave it until Allah makes it victorious or I die doing it.'

The Messenger of Allah wept, then rose and turned away. Abu Talib called out to him, 'Turn round, nephew!'

The Messenger of Allah returned. Abu Talib told him, 'Nephew, go and say whatever you like. By Allah, I will never surrender you to anyone.'

The Quraysh torture the Muslims

The Messenger of Allah continued to call people to

Allah and the Quraysh despaired of both him and Abu Talib. Their anger descended on those of their fellow tribesmen who had become Muslims and were defenceless.

Every clan targeted those who had become Muslims. They began to imprison them and torture them with beatings, hunger and thirst, even leaving them exposed on the sun-baked ground of Makkah when the heat was most intense.

Bilal, an Abyssinian, who had become a Muslim, was taken out on to the plain of Makkah by his master Umayyah ibn Khalaf and left flat on his back in the midday heat. His master ordered that a huge stone be placed on his chest and declared, 'By Allah, this stone will not be removed until you die or reject Muhammad and worship al-Lat and al-'Uzza.'

While he was suffering, Bilal would only say, 'God is One! God is One!'

Abu Bakr as-Siddiq (may Allah be pleased with him) passed by when he was lying there. He gave Umayyah a black slave who was stronger and sturdier in exchange for Bilal and he set Bilal free.

The Banu Makhzum took out 'Ammar ibn Yasir and his mother and father, who were all Muslims, into the midday heat. They tortured them by leaving them exposed to the midday sun of Makkah. The Messenger of Allah passed by them and said reassuringly, 'Fortitude, family of Yasir! You have the promise of Paradise.'

They endured their persecution until 'Ammar's mother was killed because she refused to reject Islam.

Mus'ab ibn 'Umayr was a handsome young man of Makkah whose mother was very wealthy and dressed him well. He heard that the Messenger of Allah was preaching in the house of Arqam ibn Abi'l-Arqam. After hearing about Islam, he became a Muslim. He concealed his religious beliefs because he feared the reaction of his mother and his family and he kept secret his visits to the Messenger of Allah.

However, 'Uthman ibn Talhah saw him praying and reported it to Mus'ab's family. He was seized and imprisoned. He was denied freedom until he was able to leave for Abyssinia in the first *hijrah*. When he returned with the other Muslim refugees, he was a changed man. His mother refrained from censuring him, once she saw his piety and destitution.

Some of the Muslims were under the protection of the Quraysh noblemen who were idolworshippers. 'Uthman ibn Maz'un was protected by al-Walid ibn al-Mughirah until he felt ashamed of what he was accepting. He dismissed al-Walid's offer of patronage, saying that he wanted the protection of none but Allah.

A heated conversation between him and one of the idolworshippers ended up with 'Uthman getting a black eye. Al-Walid ibn al-Mughirah, who was nearby, saw what had happened. He exclaimed, 'By Allah, nephew, your eye would not have suffered like that if you had been well-protected.'

'No, by Allah,' 'Uthman said, 'my good eye needs to suffer the same as happened to its fellow for the sake of Allah. I am under a protection which is stronger and more powerful than any you could give me, O Abu 'Abd Shams!'

The Quraysh attack the Messenger of Allah

The Quraysh were unable to divert these young Muslims from their religion and the Messenger of Allah remained defiant. The Quraysh became so irritated by their helplessness that the more foolish among them started to attack the Messenger of Allah. They even accused him of sorcery, divining and madness. They left no stone unturned in their efforts to harm him.

One day when the Quraysh nobles had met in the *Hijr,* the Messenger of Allah appeared and passed by them doing *tawaf* of the Ka'bah. They called out disparagingly to him three times. He stopped and spoke to them, 'Company of Quraysh, are you listening? By the One who has my soul in His hand, I have brought you slaughter.'

Shocked by these words, the people fell silent. Realizing that they had been rude, they began to speak to him more pleasantly.

The next day the Messenger of Allah appeared again but quickly they surrounded him and attacked him all together. One of them took hold of his cloak. Abu Bakr (may Allah be pleased with him) stood up weeping and cried, 'Would you kill a man just for saying: My Lord is Allah?'

When Abu Bakr returned later that day however, they attacked him and tore out some of his hair and dragged him along by his beard.

On another occasion when the Messenger of Allah went out everyone he met, both free men and slaves, ignored him or tried to hurt him. He returned home and wrapped himself up warmly because he was so distressed by what had happened to him. Allah revealed to him, *'O you enshrouded, rise up and warn!'* (74: 1)

The Quraysh attack Abu Bakr

One day Abu Bakr boldly invited the idolworshippers to turn towards Allah and His Messenger. Furious, they fell upon him, beating him and trampling on him. 'Utbah ibn Rabi'ah beat him on the face with a pair of sandals until his face was so swollen that his cheeks could not be distinguished from his nose.

The Banu Taym carried the unconscious Abu Bakr home. They were certain that he was going to die. In the late afternoon he woke up and asked, 'How is the Messenger of Allah?'

His relations rebuked him as he had shown concern for the man on whose account he had been beaten up. They left him alone with his mother Umm Khayr who had not as yet become a Muslim. Then Umm Jamil, who had become a Muslim, approached him and he asked her about the Messenger of Allah. She reported, 'He is well and safe.'

'By Allah,' he said, 'I will not taste food or drink until I see the Messenger of Allah!'

When it was dark and everything had calmed down, Umm Jamil and Umm Khayr took him to the Messenger of Allah who showed great tenderness towards him. He made supplication for Abu Bakr's mother and called her to Allah. She became a Muslim too.

The Quraysh are confused

The Quraysh were confused about the Messenger of Allah. They did not know how to cope with the problem of visitors from afar listening to him in Makkah. They asked the advice of al-Walid ibn al-Mughirah, an old man of some experience. It was at the time of the pilgrimage. Al-Walid said, 'Men of the Quraysh! It is the time of the festival and the delegations of the Arabs will be coming to you. They have already heard about this companion of yours. Therefore agree on one opinion about him and do not disagree so that you contradict and refute each other.'

They had a long discussion with much give and take but Al-Walid was not pleased with their conclusion and criticized it. They came back to him to ask, 'What then do you say, Abu 'Abd Shams?'

'The nearest thing to the truth is your saying that he is a magician who has brought a kind of magic that separates a man from his father, a man from his brother, a man from his wife, and a man from his tribe.'

The gathering then broke up and the Quraysh began to sit by the paths used by the people coming to the festival. They warned everyone who passed to keep clear of the Messenger of Allah and gave their reasons.

The Quraysh step up their hostilities

The Quraysh treated the Messenger of Allah harshly, ignoring the fact that he was a relative and deserved their respect.

One day while the Prophet was prostrating in the mosque surrounded by some of the Quraysh, 'Uqbah ibn Abi Mu'ayt threw the innards of a slaughtered animal on to the Prophet's back but he did not even lift his head. His daughter Fatimah came and removed them, cursing those who had committed the evil deed and the Prophet cursed them as well.

Another time, while the Prophet was praying in the *Hijr* of the Ka'bah, 'Uqbah ibn Abi Mu'ayt tried to throttle him with his own clothes. Abu Bakr grabbed 'Uqbah's shoulder and pulled him from the Prophet, saying, 'Would you kill a man just for saying, "My Lord is Allah"?'

Hamzah ibn 'Abdu'l-Muttalib accepts Islam

One day Abu Jahl passed by the Messenger of Allah at Safa hurling insults and cursing him, but when the Messenger of Allah ignored him, he left him alone.

Soon afterwards Hamzah ibn 'Abdu'l-Muttalib arrived on the scene, returning from the hunt, carrying his bow. He was the strongest of the Quraysh and the most courageous. A slavewoman of 'Abdullah ibn Jud'an told him what had happened to the Messenger of Allah. Hamzah was filled with rage. He entered the mosque and saw Abu Jahl sitting with his friends. He went towards him until he was standing over him, raised his bow and hit him with it, giving him a nasty head wound. Then he said, 'Do you insult him when I follow his religion? I say what he says.'

Abu Jahl was silent and Hamzah became a Muslim. That was a great blow to the Quraysh because Hamzah was widely respected and his courage was legendary.

'Utbah and the Messenger of Allah

When the Quraysh saw that the Companions of the Messenger of Allah were increasing in number, 'Utbah ibn Rabi'ah suggested that he go to the Messenger of Allah and try to patch up their differences. If the Quraysh made some concessions, he might agree to leave off his mission. 'Utbah was given permission to negotiate on their behalf. He went to the Messenger of Allah and sat down beside him. 'Nephew,' he said, 'you know your standing among us, but you have brought a matter of grave concern to your people. You have divided their community, made fun of their customs, criticized their gods and their religion and declared some of their ancestors to be unbelievers. Now, listen to me. I will make some proposals for you to examine and perhaps you will accept some of them.'

The Messenger of Allah said, 'Speak, Abu'l-Walid. I am listening.'

'Nephew,' 'Utbah continued, 'If you want money by this business, we will collect some of our property and make you the wealthiest among us. If you want honour, we will make you our chief so that every decision is yours. If you want a kingdom, we will make you our king. If you are possessed by a ghost of a *jinn* that you cannot drive away from yourself, we will find skilful doctors to help you. We will spend our wealth on it till you are cured.'

When 'Utbah had finished, the Messenger of Allah asked, 'Have you finished, Abu'l-Walid?'

'Yes.'

'Then listen to me.'

'I will,' said 'Utbah.

Then the Messenger of Allah recited some verses from *Surah Fussilat*. 'Utbah listened intently, putting his hands behind his back and leaning on them. When the Messenger of Allah reached the place mentioning prostration, he prostrated and then said, 'You have heard what you have heard, Abu'l-Walid. It is now up to you.'

'Utbah returned to his companions who commented, 'Abu'l-Walid has come back with a different expression on his face to the one he went with.'

When he sat down beside them, they asked him what had happened.

'By Allah!' he said, 'I have heard words the like of which I have never heard before. By Allah, it is neither poetry nor magic nor soothsaying. O men of Quraysh! Obey me! Leave this man alone with what he has. Be considerate towards him and don't interfere.'

'By Allah,' they said, 'He has bewitched you with his tongue, Abu'l-Walid!'

'This is my opinion about him,' he replied. 'You do as you see fit.'

The Muslims' *hijrah* to Abyssinia

When the Messenger of Allah saw the persecution to which his Companions were subjected and from which he could not protect them, he suggested to them, 'If you were to go to Abyssinia, you would find a king there who does not wrong anyone. It is a friendly land and you could stay there until Allah grants us relief.'

A group of Muslims left for Abyssinia and it was the first *hijrah* in Islam. Ten men, over whom 'Uthman ibn Maz'un was in charge (may Allah be pleased with him), went first. Then Ja'far ibn Abi Talib departed and other Muslims followed them. Some took their families and some went alone. In all eighty-three made the *hijrah* to Abyssinia.

The Quraysh pursue the Muslims

The Quraysh were even more annoyed when they saw that the Muslims were safe and secure in Abyssinia. They sent 'Abdullah ibn Abi Rabi'ah and 'Amr ibn al-'As ibn Wa'il there bearing gifts collected for the Negus and his generals. The choicest goods of Makkah were used to try to influence the Abyssinians in their favour. The delegation won over the generals who were pleased with their gifts and they were able to speak to the king. They told him, 'Some of our foolish fellows have taken refuge in your majesty's dominions. They have abandoned the religion of their people, but have not entered your religion. They have brought an invented religion which neither we nor you know. The nobles of our people – their fathers, uncles and clans – have sent us to ask you to return them to us. They are closest to them and know them best.'

The generals added, 'They are speaking the truth, O King. Hand them over to them.'

However, the Negus became angry and refused to accept what they said. He would not surrender anyone who had taken refuge with him in his realm. He swore by Allah and summoned the Muslims. He also summoned his bishops. He said to the Muslims, 'What is it that you have abandoned the religion of your people for, yet not entered into my religion nor any other religion?'

Ja'far ibn Abi Talib defines Islam

Ja'far ibn Abi Talib, the cousin of the Messenger of Allah, rose to explain:

> O King! we were a people of ignorance who worshipped idols, ate dead animals, committed abominations, broke off ties of kinship, treated our neighbours badly, and the strong among us abused the weak. We were like that until Allah sent a Messenger to us. We knew his noble birth, his honesty, trustworthiness and decency. He called us to proclaim the oneness of Allah and to worship Him and to renounce the stones and idols which we and our fathers were worshipping. He commanded us to speak the truth, to be faithful, to maintain ties of kinship, to be good to neighbours and to refrain from crimes and bloodshed. He has forbidden us abomi-

nations, lies, taking property from orphans and slandering chaste women. He has commanded us to worship Allah alone and not to associate anything with Him and to pray, give *zakat* and fast.

He enumerated the other commands of Islam. Then he continued:

So we have affirmed him and believed in him and have followed him in whatever he brought from Allah. We worship Allah alone and do not associate anything with Him. We consider unlawful what he has told us is unlawful and lawful what he has told us is lawful. For this reason alone our people have attacked us, tortured us and forced us from our religion. They intend to make us revert to the worship of idols instead of praising Allah Almighty. They want us to consider lawful the evil actions which we used to consider lawful.

When they tortured us and hemmed us in, and came between us and our religion, we left for your kingdom, choosing you because we needed your protection. We hoped that we would be treated fairly while we were with you, O King!

The Negus listened to all of this patiently. Then he asked, 'Do you have with you anything your companion brought from Allah?'

'Yes,' said Ja'far.

'Then recite it to me.'

Ja'far recited the beginning of *Surah Maryam*. The Negus wept until his beard was wet and the bishops wept until their books were damp with their tears.

The Qurayshi mission fails

Then the Negus said, 'This and what 'Isa brought have come from the same source.'

He turned to the deputation of Quraysh, saying, 'Go! By Allah, I will never hand them over to you.'

The next morning 'Amr ibn al-'As went to the Negus with a shrewd plan. 'O King, they say terrible things about 'Isa son of Maryam!'

The King turned to the Muslims and said, 'What do you say about 'Isa ibn Maryam?'

'We say about him what our Prophet (may Allah bless him and grant him peace) brought,' Ja'far ibn Abi Talib replied. 'That he was the servant of Allah, His Messenger, His Spirit and His word which He cast to the blessed Virgin Maryam.'

The Negus took a stick from the ground and said, 'By Allah, 'Isa ibn Maryam did not add to what you have said by so much as the length of this stick!'

He treated the Muslims with honour and gave them security. The two Qurayshi messengers had to leave in disgrace.

'Umar ibn al-Khattab accepts Islam

Allah then supported the Muslims by the Islam of 'Umar ibn al-Khattab al-'Adawi al-Qurashi. He was an imposing man, broad-shouldered, tall and brave. The Messenger of Allah wanted him to become a Muslim and prayed for him to be guided that way.

His sister, Fatimah bint al-Khattab had become a Muslim together with her husband, Sa'id ibn Zayd. They were concealing their Islam from 'Umar because of his violent nature. They knew he was against Islam and the Muslims. Khabbab ibn al-Aratt used to come to Fatimah to read the Qur'an to her.

One day 'Umar went out angrily swinging his sword to find the Messenger of Allah who was with his Companions. He had heard that they were in a house at Safa. On his way he met Nu'aym ibn 'Abdullah, who belonged to 'Umar's people the Banu 'Adi, and who was already a Muslim.

'Where are you going, 'Umar?' he asked.

'I am going to find Muhammad,' he replied, 'He has divided the Quraysh, mocked their traditions, criticized their religion and abused their gods. I am going to kill him.'

'You deceive yourself, 'Umar,' Nu'aym retorted. 'Shouldn't you go back to your own family and put their affairs in order first?'

'What do you mean, my family?'

'By Allah, your brother-in-law and cousin Sa'id ibn Zayd and your sister Fatimah bint al-Khattab have become Muslims and are following Muhammad in his religion. You had better deal with them first.'

'Umar returned to his sister and brother-in-law. Khabbab ibn al-Aratt was with them, holding a page from *Surah Ta Ha* which he was reading to them. When they heard 'Umar's footsteps, Khabbab hid in a small room in the house while Fatimah took the page and concealed it beneath her clothing. While he was approaching the house, 'Umar had heard Khabbab reciting, so he demanded, 'What is this gibberish?'

'Nothing,' they answered. 'What did you hear?'

'By Allah!' he shouted angrily, 'I have heard that you are following Muhammad in his religion!'

'Umar then started to attack his brother-in-law Sa'id ibn Zayd. His sister Fatimah rose to hold him back from her husband but he hit her and wounded her.

When he did that, his sister and brother-in-law told him, 'Yes, we have become Muslims and we believe in Allah and His Messenger, so do what you think best.'

When 'Umar saw blood on his sister, he regretted what he had done. He even admired her courage. 'Show me that page I heard Khabbab reading,' he said. 'Let me see what Muhammad has brought.'

'Umar was one among a few Quraysh who could read and write, but when she heard what he wanted, his sister answered, 'We are afraid to give it to you.'

'Do not be afraid,' he said and he promised not to destroy it.

When she heard that, she longed for 'Umar to become a Muslim. She said to him, 'Brother, you are unclean from your idolworship and only the purified may touch it.'

'Umar got up and washed and then she gave him the page bearing the passage from *Surah Ta Ha*. After reading only a few lines, he exclaimed, 'How noble and sublime are these words!'

When Khabbab heard that, he came out from hiding to say, ' 'Umar! By Allah, I hope that Allah has singled you out by the prayer of His Prophet. I heard him say last night, "O Allah, strengthen Islam with Abu'l-Hakam ibn Hisham (Abu Jahl) or 'Umar ibn al-Khattab!" Come to God! Come to God, O 'Umar!'

At that 'Umar said, 'Khabbab, guide me to Muhammad so that I can go to him and become a Muslim.'

'He is in a house at Safa,' Khabbab said, 'with some of his Companions.'

'Umar put on his sword and went to find the Messenger of Allah. He knocked on the door. When they heard his voice, one of the Companions of the Messenger of Allah got up and looked through a crack in the door. He saw 'Umar wearing his sword. In alarm, he returned to report, 'Messenger of Allah, it is 'Umar ibn al-Khattab with his sword on!'

Hamzah ibn 'Abdu'l-Muttalib said, 'Let him in. If his intentions are peaceful, we will treat him well. If not, we will kill him with his own sword.'

The Messenger of Allah said, 'Let him in,' and rose to meet 'Umar as he reached the middle of the room. He seized his cloak and dragged him along violently, saying, 'What has brought you here, Ibn al-Khattab? By Allah, I do not think that you will stop until Allah sends down a calamity upon you.'

'Messenger of Allah,' 'Umar replied, 'I have come to you to tell you that I believe in Allah and His Messenger and what has come from Allah.'

The Messenger of Allah said, *'Allahu Akbar'* so loudly that the Companions in the house knew that 'Umar had become a Muslim.

The Muslims' confidence increased when 'Umar became a Muslim as it had when Hamzah before him had become a Muslim.

News that 'Umar was a Muslim quickly spread among the Quraysh. They were very annoyed. They took up their swords against him but 'Umar fought back. The Quraysh valued their lives too much to pick quarrels with him so they decided to leave him alone.

The Quraysh boycott the Banu Hashim

Islam began to spread among the tribes. The Quraysh were so concerned that they decided to write a document containing a ban on the Banu Hashim and Banu al-Muttalib. They declared that they would not marry the women of these clans or give any in marriage to them, or sell them any goods or buy anything from them. The Quraysh displayed the parchment announcing the ban inside the Ka'bah in order to give it authority.

In the *She'b Abi Talib*

When the Quraysh did that, the Banu Hashim and Banu al-Muttalib gathered round Abu Talib and joined him in his quarters in a narrow valley of Makkah. It was the seventh year of prophethood. However, Abu Lahab ibn 'Abdu'l-Muttalib left the Banu Hashim and aligned himself with the Quraysh.

For many months the Banu Hashim lived in misery. The boycott was so rigorously applied and food was so scarce that they had to eat the leaves of trees. Their hungry children's cries could be heard all over the valley. The Quraysh told the merchants not to sell any goods to them. Prices were increased to prevent them from buying even essentials.

They remained in that state for three years. Apart from some kind Qurayshi people who secretly sent food to them they were totally abandoned. The Messenger of Allah was in the same predicament but he continued to call his people to Allah night and day, secretly and openly and the Banu Hashim remained patient.

The boycott ends

A group of fair-minded Quraysh, led by Hisham ibn 'Amr ibn Rabi'ah, hated this unfair boycott. Hisham was highly respected among his people. He contacted some men of the Quraysh whom he knew to be kind-hearted and considerate. He told them it was shameful to allow such tyranny to continue. He asked them to abandon the unjust contract. When he had persuaded five men to agree, they met together to work towards this end. When the Quraysh were assembled the next day, Zuhayr ibn Abi Umayyah, whose mother was 'Atikah bint 'Abdu'l-Muttalib, faced the people and demanded, 'People of Makkah! Do we eat and clothe ourselves while the Banu Hashim are perishing, unable to buy or sell? By Allah, I will not sit down until this unjust document is torn up!'

Abu Jahl entered the discussion to disagree but no one supported him. Al-Mut'im ibn 'Adi went to the Ka'bah to tear the document down. He found that insects had eaten it all except for the words, 'In Your name, O Allah.' The Prophet had already told Abu Talib that Allah had given white ants power over the document. Now it was declared invalid.

The deaths of Abu Talib and Khadijah

Soon after the end of the boycott, in the tenth year of prophethood, Abu Talib and Khadijah died. They had been good companions noted for their loyalty, support, and devotion. Abu Talib, however, never became a Muslim. At this time, troubles fell on the Messenger of Allah one after another.

Islam spreads

At-Tufayl ibn 'Amr ad-Dawsi came to Makkah. He was a noble man, a poet, and intelligent. The Quraysh warned him against the Messenger of Allah. As a result, he was afraid to go near him to listen to him.

'By Allah,' At-Tufayl said, 'they kept at me until I decided not to listen to him at all nor to speak with him, to the extent that I stuffed my ears with cotton. I went to the mosque and the Messenger of Allah was standing there praying at the Ka'bah. I stood near him and Allah had decided that I should hear some of his words. I heard some good words and said to myself, "By Allah, I am an intelligent man, a poet. The difference between good and evil is not concealed from me. Why should I not listen to what this man says? If what he brings is good, I will accept it. If it is evil, I will leave it." '

At-Tufayl met the Messenger of Allah in his house and told him what had happened. The Messenger of Allah offered him Islam and recited the Qur'an to him. At-Tufayl became a Muslim and returned to his people to call them to Islam. He refused to live with his family until they all became Muslims. Eventually the whole tribe of Daws turned to Islam.

The journey to Ta'if

After Abu Talib's death, the Messenger of Allah suffered more than ever before. The Quraysh had been restrained during the lifetime of Abu Talib but now they stepped up their victimization campaign. One even accosted him and showered dust on his head.

When the insults from the Quraysh became unbearable and they refused to have anything to do with Islam, the Messenger of Allah went to Ta'if to ask help of the Thaqif people and to call them to Islam. He hoped they would be sympathetic to his call.

On arriving in Ta'if, he went to the leaders and nobles of Thaqif, talked with them and called them to Allah. They, however, were rude to him and ridiculed him. They incited the town's riff-raff to shout insults at him and stone him. He retired, distressed, to the shade of a palm-tree where he sat down. Nowhere had he encountered worse treatment than that which he received at the hands of the idolworshippers in Ta'if.

The townspeople formed a line on either side of his path. When he passed they stoned him until he was bleeding. His feet were streaming with blood. He was so dejected that he complained to Allah of his helplessness and pitiable state. He sought refuge with Allah, pleading:

> O Allah, I complain to you of my weakness, lack of resources and humiliation before men. You are the Most Merciful, You are the Lord of the oppressed and You are my Lord. To whom will You entrust me? To someone far away who will frown on me or to an enemy to whom You have given power over me? If You are not angry with me, I do not care, but Your favour is better for me. I seek refuge with the light of Your face which illuminates the darkness, and by which the affairs of this world and the Next are put in order, from having Your anger descend on me or Your wrath fall upon me. I repent to You, seeking Your forgiveness and Your favour until You are well-pleased. There is no power nor strength except by Allah.

Allah sent the angel of the mountains to ask if he wanted him to bring together the two mountains between which Ta'if lay. The Messenger of Allah replied, 'No, for I hope that Allah will bring forth from them those who will worship Allah alone and not associate anything with Him.'

When 'Utbah ibn Rabi'ah and Shaybah ibn Rabi'ah saw his distress, they were moved with compassion. They called a Christian slave of theirs named 'Addas and told him to take a bunch of grapes to him. As 'Addas carried out his orders he noticed the kindness of the Messenger of Allah. He was so impressed that he became a Muslim.

The Messenger of Allah returned from Ta'if to Makkah where his people were even more opposed to him than they had been previously.

The ascent to the heavens

At this time the Messenger of Allah travelled by night from the Masjid al-Haram to the Masjid al-Aqsa. From there he was transported into the proximity to Allah that He wished him to experience. He travelled through the heavens, witnessed the signs of Allah and met the earlier Prophets.

'His eye swerved not nor swept aside. He saw one of the greatest signs of his Lord.' (53: 17–18)

He received generous hospitality from Allah and solace and compensation for the distress he had endured in Ta'if.

Next morning, he told the Quraysh what had happened to him. They rejected it, thinking him mad, calling him a liar and mocking him. Abu Bakr said, 'By Allah, if he said it, he has spoken the truth. What makes you wonder at it? By Allah, he tells me that news comes to him from heaven to the earth in any hour of the night or day and I believe him, and that is more unlikely than what you are astounded by.'

During the Ascent, Allah made fifty prayers each day obligatory for his *Ummah*. The Messenger continued to ask Allah to reduce the number of prayers until He reduced them to five prayers each day. Allah decreed that all who perform their prayers with sincerity and in expectation of a reward will receive the reward of fifty prayers.

The Messenger of Allah offers himself to the tribes

The Messenger of Allah contacted members of various Arab tribes when they came to Makkah during their festivals. He explained the beliefs of Islam to them and asked them to protect him from his enemies, saying,

'O people! I am your Messenger of Allah. He commands you to worship Him and not associate anything with Him and to abandon the worship of those you consider equal with Him. He commands you to believe in Him and confirm Him and to protect me so that I may make clear what Allah has sent to me.'

When the Messenger of Allah finished speaking, Abu Lahab usually got up to say, 'O people! This man calls on you to abandon al-Lat and al-'Uzza and your allies among the *jinn* for this innovation and misguidance he has brought! Do not obey him and do not listen to him!'

The Ansar accept Islam

While the Messenger of Allah was at 'Aqabah during the festival he met a group of the Khazraj of Yathrib and called them to Allah, the Mighty and Exalted. He offered them Islam and recited the Qur'an to them.

They were neighbours of the Jews in Madinah and had heard mention of a Prophet who was about to come. They said to each other, 'People! By Allah, you know that he must be the Prophet whom the Jews have promised you. Don't let them get to him before us.'

They accepted his teachings and became Muslims, saying, 'We have left our people and no people are more rent by enmity and evil as they are! Perhaps Allah will join us together by means of you. We will go to them and call them to this religion which we have accepted from you. If Allah gathers them to you, then no man will be mightier than you.'

They went back to their land having confirmed their faith. When they came to Madinah, they mentioned the Messenger of Allah to their brothers and called them to Islam. News soon spread among them until there was no house of the Ansar in which the Messenger of Allah was not discussed.

The First Pledge of 'Aqabah

The following year, twelve Ansar attended the festival in Makkah. They met the Messenger of Allah and gave him their pledge, the First Pledge of 'Aqabah, that they would believe in one God, abstain from theft, fornication and killing children, and obey him in what was right and proper.

When they left, the Messenger of Allah sent Mus'ab ibn 'Umayr with them. He commanded him to read the Qur'an to them, to preach Islam and to instruct them in the religion. He also led them in prayers. He was called 'The

Reader' in Madinah where he stayed with As'ad ibn Zurarah.

Islam spreads throughout Madinah

Islam began among the people of the Aws and the Khazraj in Madinah. Sa'd ibn Mu'adh and Usayd ibn Hudayr became Muslims. They were the leaders of their people, the Banu 'Abdu'l-Ashhal of Aws. They were convinced of the truth because of the wisdom and kindness of those who had become Muslims before them, particularly by the excellent presentation of Islam by Mus'ab ibn 'Umayr. All the people of the Banu 'Abdu'l-Ashhal became Muslims, and not a household of the Ansar remained in which some men and women had not accepted the faith.

The Second Pledge of 'Aqabah

Mus'ab ibn 'Umayr returned to Makkah the following year and a number of the Muslim Ansar accompanied those of their people making *hajj* who were still idolworshippers. The Muslims arranged to meet the Messenger of Allah at 'Aqabah. When they had finished the *hajj,* they met in the valley near 'Aqabah late at night. There were seventy-three men and two women. The Messenger of Allah came with his uncle, al-'Abbas ibn 'Abdu'l-Muttalib who was still an idolworshipper at that time.

The Messenger of Allah talked to them, recited the Qur'an and prayed to Allah and encouraged people to become Muslims. Then he said, 'I ask for your allegiance on the basis that you protect me as you would protect your wives and children.'

They pledged their allegiance to him. They asked him to promise that he would not leave them and return to his people. The Messenger of Allah gave his promise, 'I am from you and you are from me. I will fight those you fight and will be at peace with those with whom you are at peace.'

He chose twelve leaders from among them: nine from the Khazraj and three from the Aws.

The *Hijrah* to Madinah begins

Once the Messenger of Allah had taken this pledge, the Muslims had more security and some from Makkah took refuge with the Ansar. The Messenger of Allah ordered his Companions and those Muslims who were with him in Makkah to leave for Madinah, and to join their brothers among the Ansar. He said, 'Allah has given you brothers and an abode where you will be safe.' They soon began to leave Makkah.

The Messenger of Allah, however, remained in Makkah waiting for Allah's permission to emigrate to Madinah.

The emigration of the Muslims from Makkah was not easy. The Quraysh put many obstacles in their way and subjected the emigrants to considerable stress. However, the emigrants were determined to go. They did not want to remain in Makkah. Some, including Abu Salamah, were forced to leave their wives and children behind and to travel alone. Some had to relinquish all they had earned in their lifetime. Suhayb was among those who lost all their wealth.

'Umar ibn al-Khattab, Talhah, Hamzah, Zayd ibn Harithah, 'Abdu'r-Rahman ibn 'Awf, Zubayr ibn al-

'Awwam, Abu Hudhayfah, 'Uthman ibn 'Affan and others emigrated (may Allah be pleased with them) and the emigration continued apace. None were left in Makkah with the Messenger of Allah except for those who were imprisoned or awaiting trial, apart from 'Ali ibn Abi Talib and Abu Bakr ibn Abi Quhafah.

The Quraysh's final plot fails

When the Quraysh saw that the Messenger of Allah had Companions and helpers in Madinah over whom they had no power, they were alarmed about his departure. They knew that if that happened, they would have no means to stop him. So they assembled in the Dar an-Nadwah, the house of Qusayy ibn Kilab which the Quraysh used when decision-making. The Quraysh nobles consulted one another on what to do about the Messenger of Allah.

They finally agreed that each tribe would provide a young warrior and together they would attack the Messenger of Allah, each man striking a blow. That way responsibility for his death would be divided among the tribes and the Banu 'Abd Manaf would not be able to fight them all.

Allah informed His Messenger of this plot, so he could tell 'Ali ibn Abi Talib to sleep in his bed wrapped up in his cloak, adding, 'Nothing unpleasant will happen to you.'

When the murderous gang gathered at the door intending to attack, the Messenger of Allah came out and took up a handful of dust. Allah then instantly removed their sight and the Messenger of Allah scattered the dust over their heads while reciting verses from *Surah YaSin*, '*We have covered them so that they do not see.*' (36: 9)

Someone came to them and said, 'What are you

waiting here for?'

'Muhammad,' they replied.

'May Allah disappoint you!' he said. 'By Allah, he came out earlier and went about his business.'

When they looked and saw someone sleeping on the bed they did not doubt that it was the Messenger of Allah. But in the morning when 'Ali got up from the bed, they were so embarrassed that they slunk away quietly.

The *Hijrah* of the Messenger of Allah

The Messenger of Allah went to Abu Bakr to tell him, 'Allah has given me permission to emigrate.'

Abu Bakr exclaimed, 'In company, Messenger of Allah?'

'In company,' replied the Messenger of Allah, and Abu Bakr wept for joy.

Abu Bakr brought two camels which he had in readiness for the journey and hired 'Abdullah ibn Urayqit to act as their guide. Over the years, the Messenger of Allah had developed such a reputation for honesty that the unbelieving Quraysh would deposit their valuables with him, certain that they would be safe. This day he charged 'Ali with the responsibility for returning all the property to its rightful owners.

The Cave of Thawr

The Messenger of Allah and Abu Bakr left Makkah secretly. Abu Bakr asked his son, 'Abdullah ibn Abi Bakr, to find out what people were saying about them in Makkah and he asked 'Amir ibn Fuhayrah, his freed slave, to graze his milking sheep in the daytime but to bring them to them each night. Asma' bint Abi Bakr would bring them food.

They went to the Cave of Thawr. Abu Bakr went in first to clean it up and to make sure that it was safe so that nothing could harm the Messenger of Allah. Once he was satisfied he called him in.

When they were inside Allah sent a spider to spin a web from a bush across the entrance to the cave. It concealed the fact that the Messenger of Allah and Abu Bakr had only just gone in. Allah also commanded two wild doves to fly down between the spider and the tree. They made a nest there and laid eggs. *'To Allah belong the armies of the heavens and the earth.'* (48: 4)

The idolworshippers followed the tracks of the Messenger of Allah's party, but when they reached the mountain they became confused. They climbed up the hillside passing close to the cave. However, when they saw the spider's web they said, 'If anyone had entered here, there would not be a spider's web across the opening.' Then, they rode on. Abu Bakr saw the idolworshippers coming. In alarm he said, 'Messenger of Allah, if one of them steps forward, he will see us.'

The Messenger of Allah replied, 'Why worry about two when Allah is the third?'

Allah says in the Qur'an, *'... the second of the two; when the two were in the Cave, when he said to his companion, "Grieve not. Allah is with us." '* (9: 40)

Suraqah's experience

When the Quraysh realized that the Messenger of Allah had escaped, they offered a hundred camels to anyone who handed him over, dead or alive. The Messenger of Allah remained in the cave for three days and then left with 'Amir ibn Fuhayrah who guided him along the coastal route.

Suraqah ibn Malik ibn Ju'sham was eager to get the reward offered for the Messenger of Allah. He was tracking his footsteps when his horse stumbled and he was thrown off. He refused to give up so he mounted again and rode on. His horse stumbled a second time and he fell again. Determined to capture his quarry, he rode on once more. Just as he caught sight of the Messenger of Allah, his horse stumbled a third time. Its feet sank into the sand and Suraqah fell. Then he watched as dust rose from the ground like a sandstorm in front of him.

When Suraqah saw that happen, he knew that the Messenger of Allah was under the protection of Allah. He realized that the Messenger of Allah would certainly have the upper hand over his enemies. He called out, 'I am Suraqah ibn Ju'sham. Wait for me so that I can speak to you. By Allah, I will not harm you.'

The Messenger of Allah said to Abu Bakr, 'Ask him what he wants from us.'

'Write a document for me which will be a warrant of security.'

The Messenger of Allah asked 'Amir ibn Fuhayrah to write it and Suraqah kept the piece of leather (or bone) on which it was written for many years. The Messenger of Allah, looking ahead to the day when the Persian empire would crumble, said to Suraqah, 'How will you feel when you are wearing the bracelets of Chosroes?'

And indeed that event took place. When Persia was conquered, the bracelets, belt and crown of Chosroes were brought to 'Umar. He summoned Suraqah ibn Malik and put the royal insignia on him.

Although Suraqah offered the Messenger of Allah

provisions for his journey to Madinah, they were not accepted. He only asked, 'Conceal our presence.'

A blessed man

During their journey the Messenger of Allah's party passed the tent of Umm Ma'bad al-Khuza'iyyah who had a goat which was giving no milk during the drought. The Messenger of Allah stroked its udder, invoked the name of Allah and prayed for a blessing. Milk flowed. He gave Umm Ma'bad and his Companions milk to drink until they were satisfied. Then he drank last of all. The ewe was milked a second time and her milk filled a vessel. When Abu Ma'bad returned home, his wife told him what had happened, exclaiming, 'By Allah, it could only have been a blessed man who passed by us.'

When she described the angelic stranger, he said, 'By Allah, I think it is the man whom the Quraysh are seeking.'

In Madinah

Madinah receives the Messenger of Allah

The Messenger of Allah and his party continued their journey to Quba' which is on the outskirts of Madinah. It was Monday the 12 of Rabi' al-Awwal and this date marks the beginning of the Islamic calendar.

When the Ansar heard that the Messenger of Allah had left Makkah they waited for him even more eagerly than people who are fasting wait for the new moon of the *'Id*. Every day after the Morning Prayer they went to the outskirts of Madinah to look for him. They stayed there until the heat of the summer sun forced them to seek shade. They would go back into their houses feeling very disappointed.

On the day that the Messenger of Allah arrived, the people had just gone back into their houses. The Jews had taken note of what was going on and the first person to see him was indeed a Jew. He shouted as loudly as he could to announce to the Ansar that the Messenger of Allah had arrived. Everyone went out to greet him. He and Abu Bakr, who was about the same age, were sheltering under a palm-tree. Only a few of them had seen the Messenger of Allah before so most of the people in the crowd were unable to distinguish between him and Abu Bakr. Realizing their confusion, Abu Bakr stood up to shade him with his

MADĪNAH MUNAWWARAH

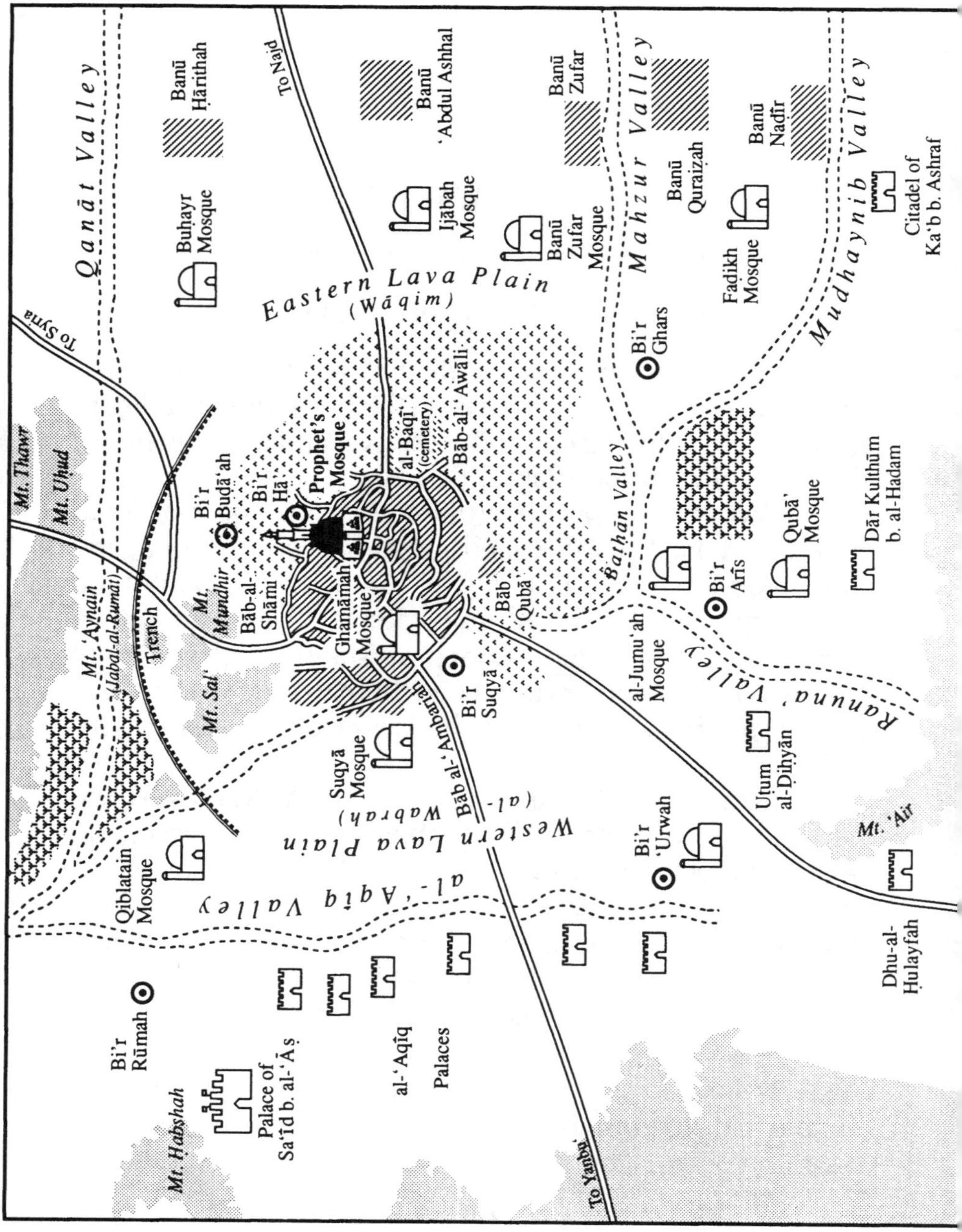

cloak from the sun, thus making it clear who was the Messenger of Allah.

The Muslims were overjoyed at the arrival of the Messenger of Allah. It was the best thing that had ever happened to them. The women and children chanted, 'This is the Messenger of Allah who has come! This is the Messenger of Allah who has come!' In their delight, the girls of the Ansar recited:

> The full moon shines down upon us from Thaniyat al-Wada'.
> We must all give our thanksgiving
>   all the while praising Allah.
> You whom Allah sends among us,
>   what you bring, we will obey.
> You've ennobled Madinah.
>   Welcome now! Guide us to His way!

Anas ibn Malik al-Ansari, a boy at that time, said, 'I saw the Messenger of Allah the day he entered Madinah. I have not seen a better or more radiant day than when he came to us in Madinah.'

The Messenger of Allah spent four days at Quba' where he established a mosque. On Friday morning, he set off again. At noon he stopped among the Banu Salim ibn 'Awf where he prayed the *Jumu'ah*. This was the first *Jumu'ah* in Madinah.

The house of Abu Ayyub al-Ansari

In Madinah the Messenger of Allah was greeted by people, all asking him to stay with them. They grabbed the halter of his camel but he said, 'Let it go its own way. It is under orders.' That happened several times. Eventually the camel stopped at the home of Banu Malik ibn an-Najjar. By herself she kneeled at a place which today marks the door of the Prophet's mosque. At that time it was used for drying dates and belonged to two orphan boys of the Banu'n-Najjar who were the Prophet's maternal uncles.

The Messenger of Allah got off his camel. Abu Ayyub Khalid ibn Zayd quickly carried his luggage into his house and the Messenger of Allah stayed with him. Abu Ayyub showed him generous hospitality and great respect. The Messenger of Allah insisted on staying on the lower floor of the house although Abu Ayyub disliked occupying the top floor above him, thinking it an insult. The Prophet, however, reassured him, saying, 'Abu Ayyub, it is more convenient for me and those who call on me that I stay on the lower floor.'

The Messenger of Allah's Mosque

The Messenger of Allah called for the two orphans who owned the date store and asked them to name a price for it, so that a mosque could be built. They said, 'We give it to you, Messenger of Allah.' He refused to accept it as a gift, however, and insisted on paying them.

The Messenger of Allah helped in the building of the mosque, carrying bricks alongside the other Muslims.

As he worked he recited, 'O Allah, the true reward is the reward of the Next World, so show mercy to the Ansar and Muhajirun!'

The Muslims were happy, reciting poetry and praising Allah.

The Messenger of Allah stayed in the house of Abu

Ayyub for seven months until his mosque and the rooms for his family were ready.

The Muhajirun joined the Messenger of Allah until none were left in Makkah except those in prison or awaiting trial. Every house of the Ansar became Muslim.

Brotherhood

The Messenger of Allah established brotherhood between the Muhajirun and the Ansar, and they were put under an obligation to assist one another. The Ansar were so eager to form a brotherhood that they had to draw lots to allocate their shares. The Ansar gave the Muhajirun authority over their homes, their furniture, their land and their animals and preferred them over themselves in every way.

An Ansari would say to a Muhajir, 'Have whichever half of my property you want to take,' and the Muhajir would say, 'May Allah bless you in your family and property! Show me the market.' From the Ansar there was great benevolence as they demonstrated their generosity to their Muslim brothers while the Muhajirun retained their self-respect.

The Prophet's covenant

The Messenger of Allah bound together the Muhajirun and the Ansar when he made a covenant with the Jews. They were confirmed in their freedom to practise religion and in their title to their wealth. Conditions were made for them and accepted from them.

The *Adhan*

When the Messenger of Allah was secure in Madinah and Islam had been strengthened, the people would join him at prayer without a call. He disliked the way the Jews and Christians used horns and bells to announce their calls to prayer. Then Allah honoured the Muslims with the *adhan*. One of them saw the method in a dream. The Messenger of Allah confirmed it and prescribed it for the Muslims. He chose Bilal ibn Rabah al-Habashi to call the *adhan*. He was the *mu'adhdhin* of the Messenger of Allah and thus became the Imam of all the *mu'adhdhins* until the end of time.

The hypocrites

Islam spread throughout Madinah and some of the rabbis and Jewish scholars also became Muslims. They included a learned rabbi named 'Abdullah ibn Salam whose acceptance of Islam annoyed other Jews. At that time the Jews were feeling anxious. They envied Islam, but at the same time they were frightened of it. Hence a group of hypocrites emerged. Their leader was 'Abdullah ibn Ubayy ibn Salul, whose power was not questioned before the arrival of Islam, but now his people were flocking to the new faith. He and others like him who were greedy for power became open enemies of Islam while others became secret hypocrites.

The *Qiblah*

The Messenger of Allah and the Muslims prayed towards Jerusalem for sixteen months after he came to

Madinah but he wanted to turn to the Ka'bah. Muslims, as Arabs, had grown up with both love and esteem for the Ka'bah. They did not consider any other house equal to it nor any *qiblah* equal to the *qiblah* of Ibrahim and Isma'il. They all would have preferred to turn towards the Ka'bah. They found that the *qiblah* towards Jerusalem was an irritation, but they declared, *'We hear and obey,'* and *'We believe it. All is from our Lord.'* They always obeyed the Messenger of Allah and submitted to the commands of Allah whether or not that was what they wanted.

First Allah tested their hearts for *taqwa* and their submission to the command of Allah. Then He turned His Messenger and the Muslims towards the Ka'bah. The Qur'an says:

'Thus We appointed you a midmost nation that you might be witnesses to the people, and that the Messenger might be a witness to you; and We did not appoint the direction you were facing, except that We might know who followed the Messenger from him who turned on his heels – it was a difficult thing except for those whom Allah has guided.' (2: 143)

The Muslims turned to the Ka'bah out of obedience to Allah and His Messenger and it became the *qiblah* of the Muslims for all time to come. Wherever they are in the world, Muslims turn their faces towards it when they pray.

The Quraysh are still hostile

When Islam was firmly established in Madinah, and the Quraysh knew that it was flourishing and spreading, they became hostile towards the Muslims. Allah commanded the Muslims to be steadfast and patient, saying, *'Restrain your hands and establish the prayer.'* (4: 77)

When the Muslims were strong and secure, they were given permission to fight but were not obliged to do so. Allah said, *'Leave is given against those whom war is made (to fight) because they were wronged. Allah is able to help them.'* (22: 39)

The first expeditions

The Messenger of Allah began to send delegations to visit other tribes and districts. Most of the time there was no war, only skirmishes. Even this much activity worried the idolworshippers but their anxiety encouraged the Muslims to emerge triumphant.

The Messenger of Allah went on the raid of Abwa', the first he himself undertook. It was followed by other raids and expeditions.

The fast

In the second year of the *hijrah,* fasting was made obligatory. Allah revealed, *'O you who believe, the fast is prescribed for you as it was prescribed for those before you – perhaps you will be godfearing.'* (2: 183)

He says, *'The month of Ramadan in which the Qur'an was sent down to be a guidance to the people and as clear signs of the Guidance and the Discrimination. Let those of you who are present at the month fast it.'* (2: 185)

The Decisive Battle of Badr

The Great Expedition of Badr took place in Ramadan, 2 A.H. Allah called this battle 'The Day of Distinguishing.' Allah says, *'If you believe in Allah and what We sent down on Our servant on the Day of Distinguishing, the day the two hosts met.'* (8: 41)

The Messenger of Allah had heard that Abu Sufyan ibn Harb, who was extremely hostile to Islam, was coming from Syria with a large trading caravan belonging to the Quraysh. They were carrying a vast quantity of wealth and merchandise. War had been declared between the Muslims and the idolworshippers and the Quraysh had been spending their wealth on fighting Islam. Their cavalry would occasionally reach the borders of Madinah and the grazing areas used by the Muslims' animals.

When the Messenger of Allah heard about this caravan, he sent Muslims to attack it. He did not attach much importance to the confrontation and did not issue a compulsory order to wage war.

When Abu Sufyan heard that the Messenger of Allah was coming towards him he sent to Makkah for help from the Quraysh to protect him from the Muslims. When this plea reached the people of Makkah, they decided that it must be serious. They prepared themselves quickly and

BATTLE OF BADR (17th RAMAḌĀN 2 A.H.)

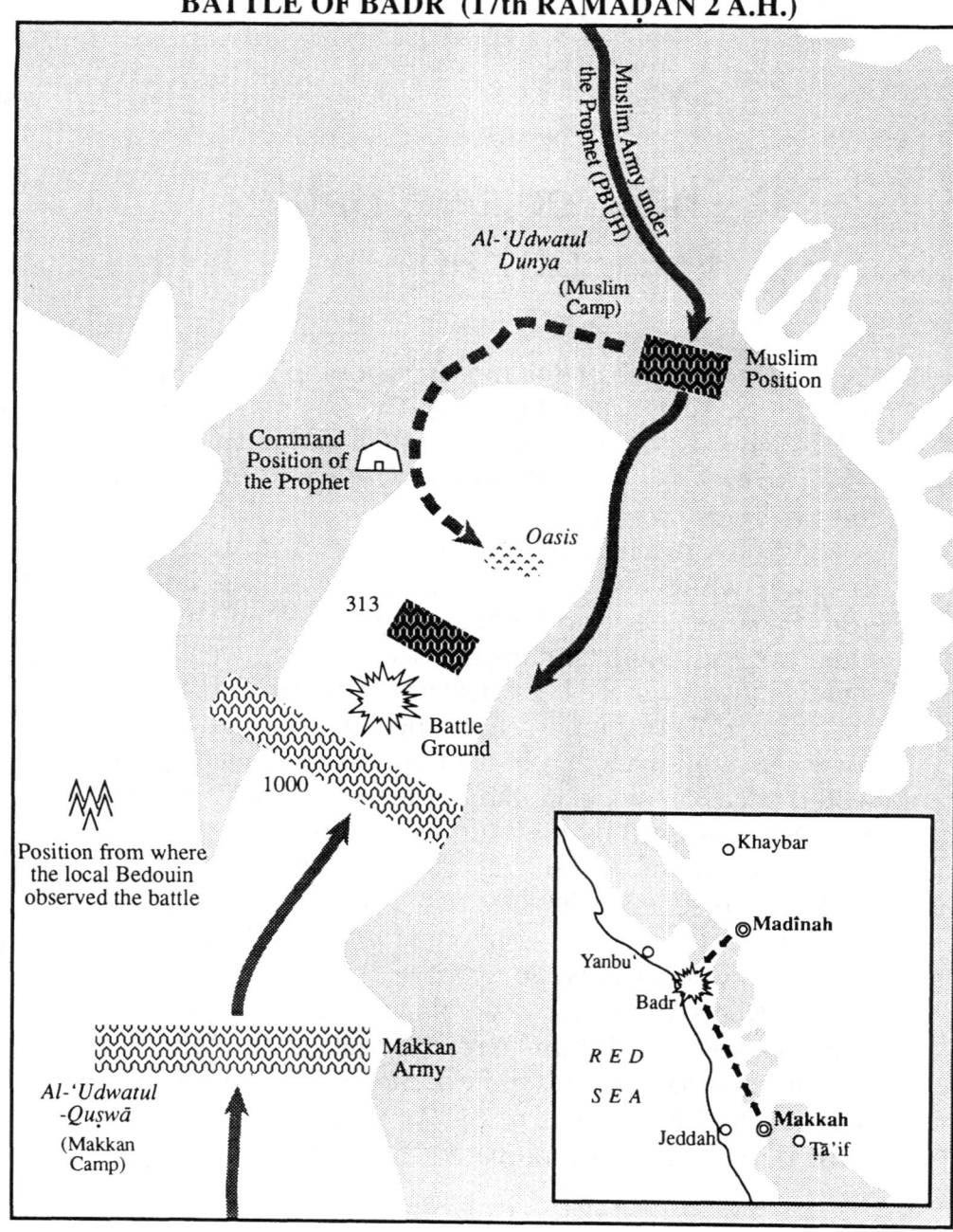

Al-'Udwatul Dunya (Muslim Camp)

Muslim Army under the Prophet (PBUH)

Muslim Position

Command Position of the Prophet

Oasis

313

Battle Ground

1000

Position from where the local Bedouin observed the battle

Makkan Army

Al-'Udwatul -Quṣwā (Makkan Camp)

Khaybar

Madīnah

Yanbuʿ

Badr

RED SEA

Jeddah

Makkah

Ṭā'if

74

departed. All of their nobles, apart from Abu Lahab, went to help and he appointed a man to take his place.

Assurance from the Ansar

When the Messenger of Allah heard that the Quraysh had set out from Makkah to stop the Muslims, he consulted his Companions. He was concerned about the Ansar because their original homage included the condition that they only defend him in their home territory. Since he resolved to leave Madinah, he wanted to know where they stood. The Muhajirun assured him of their support, but he consulted them a second time, and then a third time. The Ansar fully understood the reason why he was concerned about them. Sa'd ibn Mu'adh replied,

'It seems that you are alluding to us. Perhaps you fear that the Ansar do not think that they have to help you outside their own territory. I speak for the Ansar and answer for them. Go where you wish, join whom you wish and cut off whom you wish. Take what you wish from our property and give us what you wish. What you take from us is dearer than what you leave. Whatever you command, we will follow it. By Allah, if you were to travel until you reached Bark Ghamdan, we would go with you. By Allah, if you were to cross this sea, we would plunge into it with you.'

Al-Miqdad said, 'We do not say to you what the people of Musa said to Musa: *"Go forth, you and your Lord and do battle. We will be waiting here."* (5: 24) We will do battle on your right and on your left and in front of you and behind you.'

When the Messenger of Allah heard this, his face shone with happiness 'Be Steadfast!', he said to his Companions.

Jihad and martyrdom

When the Muslims went to Badr, a boy called 'Umayr ibn Abi Waqqas came out. He was sixteen and afraid that the Prophet would not accept him because he was too young to fight. He tried to avoid being seen but his elder brother, Sa'd ibn Abi Waqqas, asked him what he was up to.

'I was afraid that the Messenger of Allah would send me back when I wanted to go out. It might be that Allah will grant me martyrdom,' he answered.

That was indeed the case. The Messenger of Allah did want to send him back because he was so young. 'Umayr wept. His tears weakened the heart of the Messenger of Allah who allowed him to go after all. And 'Umayr was killed as a martyr during the expedition.

Disparity in numbers

The Messenger of Allah set off for Badr swiftly with three hundred and thirteen men but only two horses and seventy camels. Two or three men rode on a camel in turns without any distinction being made between a soldier and a general. The Messenger of Allah, Abu Bakr, 'Umar and the great Companions were among them.

The Prophet gave the banner to Mus'ab ibn 'Umayr, the flag of the Muhajirun to 'Ali ibn Abi Talib and the flag of the Ansar to Sa'd ibn Mu'adh.

When Abu Sufyan heard that the Muslims had set out to intercept him, he turned his caravan towards the coast. When he saw that they were safe, he sent word to the Quraysh telling them to return as there was now nothing for them to do. The Quraysh wanted to turn back, but Abu Jahl insisted on attacking. The Quraysh army numbered more than a thousand, including all the warriors, leaders and horsemen. Of the fighters the Messenger of Allah said, 'Makkah has sent you its treasures, dear and beloved ones.'

The Messenger of Allah and his Companions reached the water of Badr first. They arrived at midnight and built cisterns which they filled with water. The Messenger of Allah allowed unbelievers to drink of this water, too.

Allah sent down heavy rain that night. It prevented the idolworshippers from advancing. It was a mercy for the Muslims, however, as it made the ground smooth and the sand firm. This blessing strengthened their hearts. Allah describes the scene:

'He sent down water on you from heaven, to purify you thereby and to put away from you the defilement of Satan, and to strengthen your hearts and to confirm your feet.' (8: 11)

Preparation for battle

A shelter was built for the Messenger of Allah on a small hill overlooking the battlefield. He went down to the battlefield and began to point with his hand, saying, 'So-and-so will die here. So-and-so will die here. So-and-so will die here if Allah wills.' None of those people went any further than where he had pointed.

When the idolworshippers appeared and the two groups confronted one another, the Messenger of Allah said, 'O Allah, this is the Quraysh who have come with their vanity and their pride. They have come to fight You and deny Your Messenger.'

It was the night of Friday, 17 Ramadan. In the morning, the Quraysh advanced in their squadrons and the two groups took up positions ready for battle.

Supplication and entreaty

The Messenger of Allah organized the ranks and returned to his shelter. He and Abu Bakr went inside. The Messenger of Allah prayed. He asked for the help of Allah Whose judgement cannot be turned aside and Whose decree cannot be averted. There is no help but from Allah. He said, 'O Allah, if You let this group of men die, no one after them will worship You on the earth.'

He called out to his Lord, 'O Allah, give me the help which You promised me.'

He raised his hands to the sky until the cloak fell from his shoulders. Abu Bakr consoled and comforted him.

A confrontation

Then the Messenger of Allah went out to encourage the Muslims to fight. 'Utbah ibn Rabi'ah and his brother Shaybah and his son al-Walid stepped forward from the Quraysh. When they came forward between the opposing forces, they asked for other people to come forward as was the custom. When three youths of the Ansar went out to them they asked, 'Who are you?'

'We are from the Ansar.'

'We demand our equals. Send some of our own tribe out to us.'

The Prophet said, 'Go forward, 'Ubaydah ibn al-Harith [ibn al-Muttalib ibn 'Abd Manaf], Hamzah and 'Ali.'

'Yes, these are our equals in nobility,' they said.

'Ubaydah, the oldest man chosen, went out against 'Utbah, Hamzah against Shaybah and 'Ali against al-Walid ibn 'Utbah. Hamzah and 'Ali quickly killed their opponents. 'Ubaydah and 'Utbah exchanged blows and each of them floored the other. Hamzah and 'Ali turned their swords against 'Utbah and finished him off and carried back 'Ubaydah, who was wounded. He died a martyr.

War breaks out

The people crowded together and drew near to one another. The idolworshippers approached. The Messenger of Allah cried out, 'Arise for a Paradise as wide as the heavens and the earth!'

'Umayr ibn al-Humam al-Ansari got up, asking, 'Messenger of Allah! A Paradise as wide as the heavens and the earth?'

'Yes,' he said.

'Wonderful, wonderful, Messenger of Allah!'

'What moved you to say "Wonderful, wonderful"?'

'Nothing, by Allah, Messenger of Allah,' he said, 'except the hope that I will be among its people.'

'You are one of its people,' he was told.

'Umayr took some dates from his quiver and began to eat. 'If I live to eat these dates it will be a long life,' he suddenly said.

So he threw away the dates and ran to the battlefield. He fought the enemy until he was killed. He was the first martyr that day.

The people were steadfast, constantly remembering Allah. The Messenger of Allah fought fiercely. He fought closely with the enemy and none was braver that day. The angels brought down mercy and victory and drove back the idolworshippers.

Brothers competing in *Jihad*

The young men competed with each other as they raced for martyrdom and happiness. It was a race between friends, comrades and brothers.

'Abdu'r-Rahman ibn 'Awf said, 'I was in the ranks on the day of Badr. I turned and there were two young boys one on my right and the other on my left. I was not too happy about their position. One of them said to me, in a quiet voice that his companion could not hear, "Uncle, show me Abu Jahl." I said, "Nephew, what will you do to him?" He replied, "I have made a covenant with Allah that if I see him, I will kill him or die before him." The other boy then said the same thing to me, also keeping it from his companion.' He added, 'I was so happy to be between two men like them. I pointed Abu Jahl out to them and they attacked him like two falcons until they struck him down.'

When Abu Jahl was killed, the Messenger of Allah said, 'This Abu Jahl was the Pharaoh of this community.'

A clear victory

When the victory of the Muslims and the defeat of the idolworshippers became clear, the Messenger of Allah said, 'Allah is greater! Praise belongs to Allah Who was true to His promise, helped His slave and defeated the parties alone.'

Allah certainly spoke the truth when He said: *'Allah surely helped you at Badr when you were utterly abject. So fear Allah and perhaps you will be thankful.'* (3: 123)

The Messenger of Allah ordered the Quraysh dead to be thrown into a well. Then he stood over it and said, 'O people of the well! Have you found what Allah promised you to be true? I have certainly found that what my Lord promised me is true.'

Seventy leaders of the unbelievers were killed and another seventy captured on the Day of Badr. Six Muslims of the Quraysh and eight of the Ansar were martyred.

The Messenger of Allah divided the captives among his Companions and told them to treat them well.

He then returned to Madinah confirmed in victory. All his enemies both in the city and in surrounding areas feared him. Many more people of Madinah were encouraged to become Muslims.

In Makkah the idolworshippers mourned for their slain. Terror entered the hearts of all the Muslims' enemies.

Captives as teachers

The Messenger of Allah pardoned the captives and accepted ransom from them. He was gracious to those who had nothing and set them free. The Quraysh sent money to ransom the captives and he set them free too.

Among the captives were those who had nothing with which to ransom themselves. The Messenger of Allah allowed them to earn their freedom by teaching the children of the Ansar to write. Each prisoner taught ten Muslims. Zayd ibn Thabit was one of those who learned in this way from the captives of Badr.

The Banu Qaynuqa' were the first Jews to break the agreement they had made with the Messenger of Allah by insulting him and harming the Muslims. The Messenger of Allah then laid siege to them for fifteen days until they surrendered unconditionally. Their ally, 'Abdullah ibn

Ubayy, the head of the hypocrites, interceded for them and the Messenger of Allah raised the siege at his request. Seven hundred Jewish artisans and merchants were bearing arms on that occasion.

The Battle of Uhud

Revenge

When their heroes were defeated on the Day of Badr and the remnants of the army returned to Makkah, it was a terrible blow for the Quraysh. Men who had lost their fathers, sons and brothers approached Abu Sufyan and others who had valuable merchandise in that caravan. They wanted the profits to be used for fighting the Muslims again. The merchants agreed to their request. The Quraysh decided to conduct a new war. Poets spurred the people on with their militant verses and provoked fanatical zeal in readiness for battle.

A well-equipped Quraysh army set out from Makkah in the middle of Shawwal 3 A.H. The leaders accompanied by their wives advanced until they set up camp at the gates of Madinah. The Quraysh had mustered three thousand soldiers.

The Messenger of Allah thought that the Muslims should stay in the city and fight only if the enemy came into Madinah. 'Abdullah ibn Ubayy agreed with him but some of the Muslim men who had missed fighting at Badr said, 'Messenger of Allah, lead us out to face our enemies so that they will not think us cowards and weaklings.'

They kept urging on the Messenger of Allah until he went into his house and put on his armour. Then those who

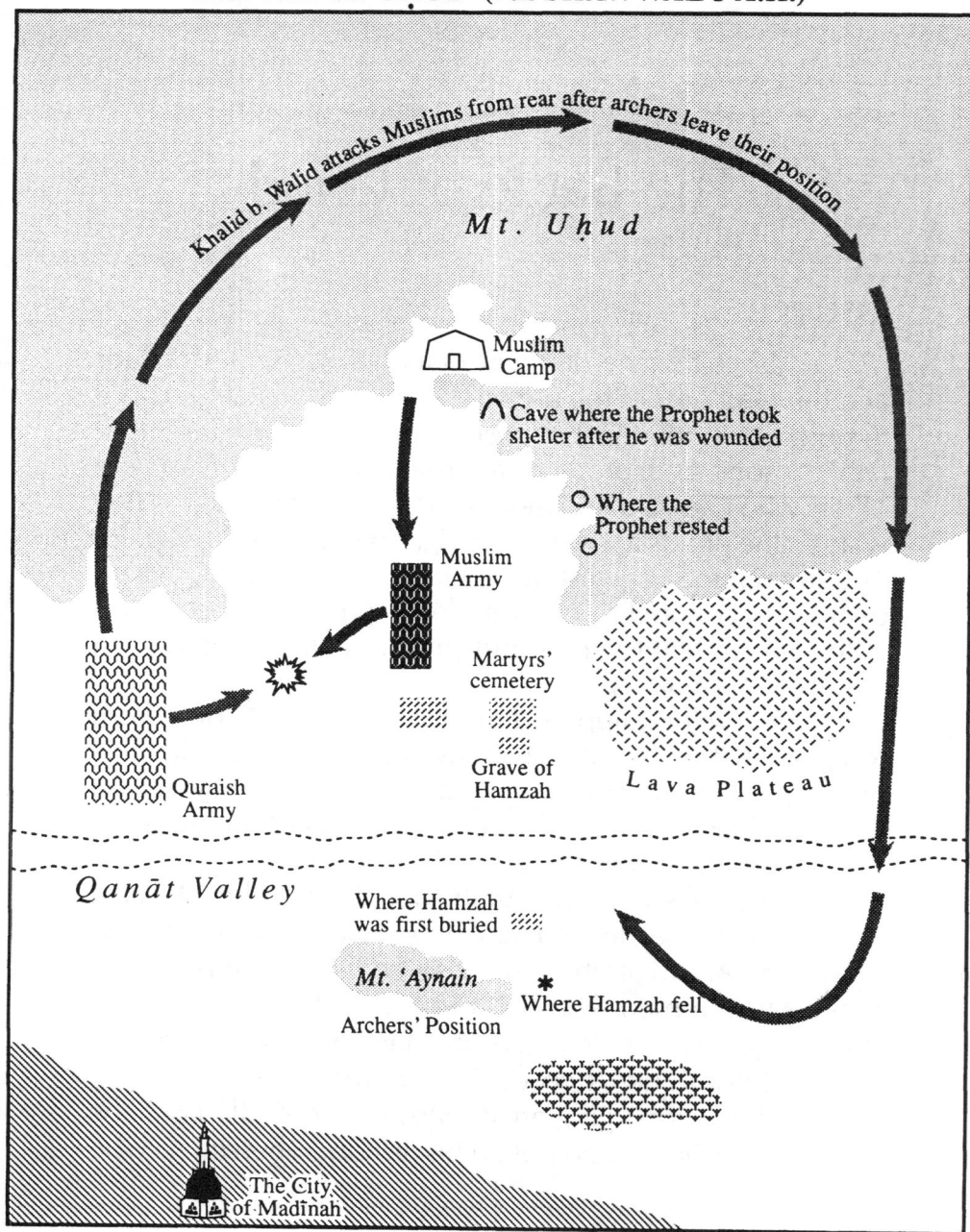

BATTLE OF UḤUD (7th SHAWWĀL 3 A.H.)

Khalid b. Walid attacks Muslims from rear after archers leave their position

Mt. Uḥud

Muslim Camp

Cave where the Prophet took shelter after he was wounded

Where the Prophet rested

Muslim Army

Martyrs' cemetery

Grave of Hamzah

Lava Plateau

Quraish Army

Qanāt Valley

Where Hamzah was first buried

Mt. 'Aynain

Where Hamzah fell

Archers' Position

The City of Madīnah

had suggested going out of the city regretted their insistence and said, 'We have persuaded you, Messenger of Allah, for which we had no right. If you wish, stay and may Allah bless you.'

The Messenger of Allah then said, 'It is not fitting that a Prophet who has put on his armour should put it aside until he has fought.'

The Messenger of Allah went out with a thousand of his Companions. When he was at ash-Shawt between Madinah and Uhud, 'Abdullah ibn Ubayy withdrew with a third of the men, saying, 'He has obeyed them and rebelled against me.'

In battle position

When the Messenger of Allah, now with seven hundred men, reached the gorge of Uhud, a mountain about three kilometres from Madinah, he took up his position saying, 'None of you should start fighting until we give the order.'

He prepared for battle. He put 'Abdullah ibn Jubayr in charge of the fifty archers, instructing them, 'Keep the cavalry away from us with arrows so that they do not come up from our rear whether the battle is going for us or against us.'

He commanded them to hold their position and not to leave it, even if they saw birds snatching the army away. He put on two coats of armour and gave the banner to Mus'ab ibn 'Umayr (may Allah be pleased with him).

Another race for *Jihad*

On the day of Uhud the Messenger of Allah sent

back a group of boys because they were too young. They included Samurah ibn Jundub and Rafi' ibn Khadij who were only fifteen years old. The father of Rafi' interceded, saying to the Messenger of Allah that his son Rafi' was a good shot, so the Prophet allowed the boy to go.

Samurah ibn Jundub who was the same age as Rafi' was presented to the Messenger of Allah who sent him back because he was too young. Samurah said, 'You gave permission to Rafi' but you sent me back. If I were to wrestle with him, I would throw him.'

They wrestled and Samurah threw Rafi' so he was given permission as well. Consequently he was able to fight in the Battle of Uhud.

The battle

The two sides faced each other and closed in. Hind bint 'Utbah stood among the women beating on drums behind the men to urge them on. A fierce battle was soon in progress. Abu Dujanah fought with the sword of the Messenger of Allah. He fought until he was deep in the enemy's ranks and killed all those in his path.

Hamzah ibn 'Abdu'l-Muttalib fought fiercely, killing many Qurayshi heroes. No one could stand against him until Wahshi, the slave of Jubayr ibn Mut'im, waited for him in ambush. He was expert at throwing the javelin and seldom missed his mark. Jubayr had promised him that he would set him free if he killed Hamzah. He had killed his uncle Tu'aymah in the Battle of Badr. Hind, the wife of Abu Sufyan who was thirsting for revenge, also encouraged him to kill Hamzah. Wahshi attacked Hamzah with his spear, striking him so hard that it pierced the lower part of his body. Hamzah fell, a martyr.

Mus'ab ibn 'Umayr fought in front of the Messenger of Allah until he was killed.

The Muslims' victory

Allah Almighty sent down His help for the Muslims. He confirmed His promise until the idolworshippers were cut off from their camp and were clearly defeated. The women turned in flight.

When the Muslim archers saw that the idolworshippers had been routed and had turned in flight to the point that they caught up with their women, they themselves left their post. They headed for the camp, certain of victory, crying, 'People! Booty! Booty!'

Their commander reminded them of the Messenger of Allah's order not to leave their post, but they did not listen. They assumed that the idolworshippers would not come back and so they left the Muslim army unprotected. Then, the cavalry of idolworshippers suddenly attacked from the rear. A shout went up, 'Muhammad has been killed!' Though the Muslims turned back straightaway, the idolworshippers seized the opportunity to counter-attack.

It was a day on which all the Muslims were sorely tested. The enemy fought their way close to the Messenger of Allah who was hit with a rock. He fell on his side, one of his front teeth was smashed, his face was scratched and his lip cut. The blood ran down his face and he wiped it away, saying, 'How can a people prosper who have stained their Prophet's face with blood while he summoned them to their Lord?'

In the confusion, many of the Muslims did not know where the Messenger of Allah was. 'Ali ibn Abi Talib took his hand and Talhah ibn 'Ubaydullah helped him to his feet.

Malik ibn Sinan, very upset, licked away the blood from his face.

The Muslims, though not put to flight, were out-manoeuvred and forced to resume the fight.

The Muslims suffered greatly from this reversal. The archers' behaviour led to the martyrdom of many strong and dedicated Companions.

The archers' failure to hold to the instructions of the Messenger of Allah and his orders not to leave their specified position is referred to in the Qur'an:

'Allah was true in His promise towards you when you blasted them by His leave; until you lost heart and quarrelled about the matter and were rebellious, after He had shown you that you longed for. Some of you there are that desire this world, and some of you there are desire the Next World. Then He turned you from them, that He might try you, and He has pardoned you and Allah is bounteous to the believers.' (3: 152)

Wonders of love and sacrifice

During the battle, two links from the metal chain-strap of the Messenger of Allah's helmet had been forced into his cheek. Abu 'Ubaydah ibn al-Jarrah removed one link from his face and a front tooth fell out; he pulled out another link and a second tooth fell out. Thus he lost both of his front teeth. Abu Dujanah had positioned himself as a shield for the Messenger of Allah. Countless arrows stuck in his back while he was leaning over him. Sa'd ibn Abi Waqqas shot arrows in defence of the Messenger of Allah who was handing him the arrows, saying, 'Shoot, may my father and mother be your ransom.'

When the eye of Qatadah ibn an-Nu'man was

injured it fell out of its socket on to his cheek. The Messenger of Allah put it back in and it was subsequently his best and sharpest eye. The frenzied idolworshippers had surged towards the Messenger of Allah, trying to achieve something Allah had not willed. Ten Companions who were protecting him were killed. Talhah ibn 'Ubaydullah shielded the Messenger of Allah from arrows with his bare hand. His fingers bled profusely and his hand became paralysed. When the Messenger of Allah wanted to climb a rock he was unable to do so because of his wounds and weakness. Talhah squatted down so that he could use him as a step. The time for the noon-prayer came and he led them in the prayer sitting down because of his wounds.

When the Muslims had been dispersed, Anas ibn an-Nadr, the uncle of Anas ibn Malik, the Messenger of Allah's servant, continued to fight on. Sa'd ibn Mu'adh asked him, 'Where are you going, Abu 'Umar?'

'Towards the scent of the Garden of Paradise, Sa'd,' he replied. 'I smell it near Uhud!'

He came upon some men of the Muhajirun and Ansar who were sitting down looking gloomy, and asked them, 'Why are you sitting here?'

'The Messenger of Allah has been killed,' they said.

'Then what use is life after him? Get up and die as the Messenger of Allah died.'

Then he went forward and fought the enemy until he was killed.

Anas (may Allah be pleased with him) said, 'We found seventy wounds on him that day. Only his sister could recognize him, and she recognized him by his fingertips.'

Ziyad ibn as-Sakan fought alongside five of the

Ansar in front of the Messenger of Allah; they were killed one by one. Ziyad fought until he was badly wounded. The Messenger of Allah said, 'Bring him to me.' He used his foot as a support for Ziyad's head. Ziyad died with his cheek on the Messenger of Allah's foot.

'Amr ibn al-Jamuh was very lame and had four young sons who used to go on expeditions with the Messenger of Allah. When they went to Uhud, he wanted to accompany the Prophet. His sons said to him, 'Allah has given you a dispensation. You stay and we will fight in your place for Allah has removed the obligation of *jihad* from you.'

'Amr came to the Messenger of Allah and said, 'These sons of mine prevent me from doing *jihad* with you. By Allah, I hope that I will be martyred and then I will walk in the Garden of Paradise with this lameness of mine.'

The Prophet replied, 'Allah has removed the duty of *jihad* from you.'

He asked his sons, 'What harm is there in letting him go?' 'Amr went with the army and was indeed blessed with martyrdom at Uhud.

Zayd ibn Thabit (may Allah be pleased with him) said, 'On the day of Uhud, the Messenger of Allah sent me to look for Sa'd ibn ar-Rabi'. "If you see him," he said, "Greet him from me and tell him, 'The Messenger of Allah says to you, "How do you feel?"' '

'I began to go among the slain and I came to him when he was breathing his last. He had seventy wounds – spear wounds, sword wounds and arrow wounds. I said, "Sa'd! The Messenger of Allah sends you his greeting and says to you, 'How do you feel?'" He said, "And peace be upon the Messenger of Allah. Say to him, 'Messenger of Allah, I can smell the scent of the Garden.' Tell my people the Ansar, 'You have no excuse with Allah if anything happens to your Prophet while you still breathe.'" He died straight after saying that.'

'Abdullah ibn Jahsh said on that day, 'O Allah, I swear to you that if I meet the enemy tomorrow and they kill me and then split my stomach open and cut off my nose and my ears and You ask me what all that was for, I will say, "For you, my Lord." '

The aftermath of battle

When the Muslims realized that the Messenger of Allah was still alive, they rushed up to one another and advanced towards the gorge. Ubayy ibn Khalaf caught up with him, saying, 'O Muhammad! I will not be spared if you are spared!' The Messenger of Allah, however, said to his Companions, 'Leave him alone.' When he came closer, the Messenger of Allah took a spear from one of his Companions, faced Ubayy and struck him in the neck causing him to sway and fall from his horse.

'Ali ibn Abi Talib filled his shield with water and Fatimah, the daughter of the Prophet, washed the blood from his face. When Fatimah saw that the water only increased the blood flow, she burnt a piece of matting and dressed the wound with the ashes until the bleeding stopped.

'A'ishah bint Abi Bakr and Umm Sulaym carried water in leather bags on their backs. They poured it into the mouths of the wounded. Repeatedly they went back for more water which Umm Sulayt drew for them.

Hind bint 'Utbah and the Quraysh women with her began to mutilate the bodies of the slain Muslims and cut off their ears and noses. She cut out Hamzah's liver and chewed it, but could not swallow it and spat it out.

When Abu Sufyan wanted to leave, he went to the top of the mountain and shouted at the top of his voice, 'The luck of war alternates. One wins today, the other tomorrow. Show your superiority, Hubal!'

The Messenger of Allah said, 'Get up, 'Umar and tell him, "Allah is the most High and Majestic. We are not the same. Our dead are in the Garden of Paradise and your dead are in the Fire!" '

Abu Sufyan retorted, 'We have 'Uzza and you do not have 'Uzza!'

The Messenger of Allah said, 'Tell him, "Allah is our Protector and you have no protector!" '

Before Abu Sufyan left, he cried out, 'Your rendezvous is Badr next year.'

The Messenger of Allah asked a Companion to say, 'Yes, it is an appointment between us.'

The Muslims searched for their dead and buried them. The Messenger of Allah grieved for Hamzah who was his uncle as well as his foster brother and who had always supported him.

A believing woman's bravery

Safiyyah bint 'Abdu'l-Muttalib came to look at Hamzah. She was his full sister. However, the Messenger of Allah told her son, az-Zubayr ibn al-'Awwam to send her back. 'She must not see what has happened to her brother.'

Az-Zubayr said to her, 'Mother, the Messenger of Allah orders you to go back.'

She asked, 'Why? I have heard that my brother has been mutilated and that it was for the sake of Allah. I assume he will be rewarded. I shall be patient if Allah is willing.'

She then went to see her brother and prayed for him, saying, 'To Allah we belong and to Him we return,' and begged forgiveness for him. Then the Messenger of Allah commanded that he be buried at Uhud.

The martyrs are buried

Mus'ab ibn 'Umayr, the Messenger of Allah's standard-bearer, was one of the wealthiest young men of the Quraysh before becoming a Muslim. Only a small piece of cloth could be found for his shroud. When his head was covered, his feet showed and when his feet were covered, his head was exposed. The Messenger of Allah advised, 'Cover his head and put *idhkhir,* herbs, on his feet.'

The Messenger of Allah put two of the dead of Uhud in a single shroud and asked, 'Which of them knew the most Qur'an?'

The one who was pointed out was put into the grave first. 'I will be a witness for them on the Day of Resurrection,' said the Messenger of Allah.

He ordered that they be buried still covered with blood, in the condition that they had fallen. They were not prayed for, neither were they washed.

A woman's joy

As they returned to Madinah, the Muslims passed by a woman of the Banu Dinar. She had lost her husband, brother and father in the battle. When she learnt of their deaths she only said, 'What has happened to the Messenger of Allah?'

The Muslims said, 'He is well, Umm so-and-so!'

She praised Allah and requested them, 'Point him out to me so that I can see him.'

When the Messenger of Allah was pointed out to her she said to him, 'Now that you are safe every misfortune is gone.'

The Muslims' desperate struggle

The idolworshippers criticized one another and their leaders, saying, 'You did not do anything. You have merely scratched the surface. You left without wiping them out.'

The Muslims were still exhausted and many were wounded. The day after Uhud, the Messenger of Allah's crier announced that they should pursue the enemy. No one should leave except those who had fought the day before. All the Muslims went out with the Messenger of Allah. None stayed behind. They reached Hamra' al-Asad about eight miles from Madinah where they camped for three days – Monday, Tuesday and Wednesday – and then returned to Madinah when there were no signs of the enemy returning.

Seventy Muslims were martyred in the Battle of Uhud, most of them Ansar (may Allah be pleased with them). Twenty-two idolworshippers were killed.

Double-crossed

In 3 A.H., some of the 'Adal and al-Qarah asked for Muslims to teach them the faith. The Messenger of Allah sent six of his Companions including 'Asim ibn Thabit, Khubayb ibn 'Adi and Zayd ibn al-Dathinah. However the tribesmen double-crossed them and killed four.

When he was captured, Zayd was taken for execution and a group of Quraysh which included Abu Sufyan ibn Harb gathered round. Abu Sufyan called out, 'I ask you by Allah, Zayd, don't you wish that Muhammad was with us now in your place so that we might cut off his head, and that you were with your family?'

Zayd replied, 'By Allah, I don't wish Muhammad to be hurt even by a thorn when I should be safe with my family.'

Abu Sufyan said, 'I have never seen a man so loved as Muhammad's Companions love Muhammad.'

Then Zayd was killed.

When Khubayb was about to be executed he asked, 'Could you let me pray two *rak'ats*?'

'Go ahead,' his captors replied.

He performed serenely two *rak'ats* and then turned and said to the people, 'By Allah, if it were not that you would think that I prolonged it out of fear of death, I would have prayed more.'

He then recited these two verses of poetry:

> I do not care if I am killed as a Muslim,
>   Whatever death I suffer is for the sake of Allah.
> It is all for Allah and if He wishes
>   He will bless the limbs which are torn apart.

An ambush

'Amir ibn Malik asked the Messenger of Allah to send a group of his Companions to teach his tribe about Islam. Seventy of the best Muslims were sent. When they reached Bi'r Ma'unah they dismounted, but the tribes of the

Banu Sulaym of 'Usayyah, Ri'l and Dhakwan ambushed them by surrounding them with their camels. When they saw what was happening, the Muslims drew their swords and fought bravely, but they were all killed except Ka'b ibn Zayd. He survived until the battle of the Ditch where he, too, was martyred.

Influential last words

When Haram ibn Milhan was killed by Jabbar ibn Sulma, his killer became a Muslim when he heard what Haram had uttered as he was dying. Jabbar explained, 'Part of the reason I became a Muslim was that on that day when I stabbed one of their men between the shoulders with a spear and saw its point come out of his chest, I heard him say, "I have won, by the Lord of the Ka'bah!" I said to myself, "What has he won? Haven't I killed the man?" I enquired from others and they told me that he meant martyrdom. "He has won, by Allah!" I replied that was the reason I became a Muslim.'

The Banu'n-Nadir are banished

The Messenger of Allah approached the Banu'n-Nadir, a large tribe of Jews, to ask for their help in paying the blood-money of two men of the Banu 'Amir who had been killed. An alliance had been made between the Banu'n-Nadir and the Banu 'Amir. Although they promised to cooperate with him, they were really plotting to assassinate him. While the Messenger of Allah was sitting by the wall of one of their houses, they discussed what to do next. 'You will never have such a good opportunity as this again. Who will go up to the top of this house and throw a rock down onto him and rid us of him?'

With the Messenger of Allah was a group of his Companions including Abu Bakr, 'Umar and 'Ali.

Allah informed His Messenger about the treacherous plan. He went straight back to Madinah and ordered the Muslims to prepare for war against the Banu'n-Nadir. Then he led them to the enemy fortress. It was in the month of Rabi' al-Awwal in 4 A.H.

The Messenger of Allah laid siege to the Jews for six nights, casting terror into their hearts. They then asked the Messenger of Allah if he would banish them from the city and spare their lives on condition that they take with them all their belongings on their camels, except their weapons. The offer was accepted and they left Madinah after destroying their houses, taking whatever their camels could carry.

The Messenger of Allah divided what property was left among the first Muhajirun.

The *Dhat ar-Riqa'* expedition

In 4 A.H. the Messenger of Allah decided to make a raid into Najd, advancing with his Companions until he reached Nakhl. They had only one camel between six of them so their feet became raw from walking. They tore their clothes into strips to bandage their feet and toes. This expedition was called *Ghazwah Dhat ar-Riqa'*, the expedition of Rags.

Though the two sides approached each other, no fighting ensued as they were too wary of each other. The Messenger of Allah led the Prayer of Fear on this occasion.

BATTLE OF THE TRENCH (DHU-AL-QA'DAH 5 A.H.)

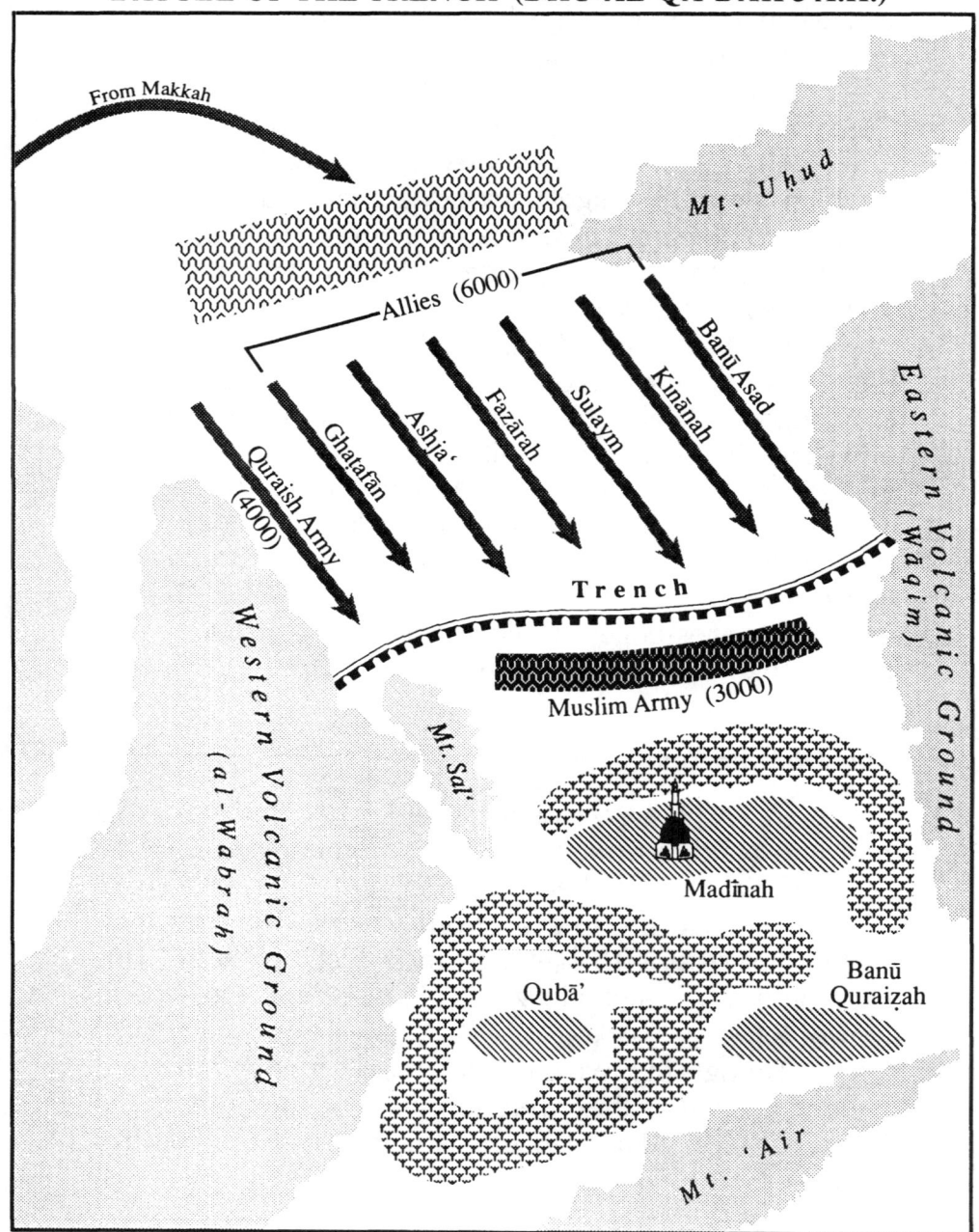

The Battle of the Ditch

The Battle of the Ditch took place in Shawwal 5 A.H. It was a decisive battle but it presented to the Muslims grave trials that they had not previously experienced. Allah says in the Qur'an:

> *When they came against you from above you and from below you, and when your eyes swerved and your hearts reached your throats, and you thought thoughts about Allah; there it was that the believers were tried, and shaken most mightily.* (33: 11)

The Jews instigated these hostilities. People from the Banu'n-Nadir and the Banu Wa'il went to the Quraysh in Makkah, calling on them to fight the Messenger of Allah. The Quraysh who had already experienced war with the Prophet were reluctant to get involved again. However, the Jewish delegation painted such a rosy picture of the outcome that they agreed to cooperate.

'We will support you,' the Jews promised, 'until you obliterate him.'

That delighted the Quraysh. They were eager to carry out the Jews' ideas. They gathered their forces and prepared for battle. The Jewish delegation then went to the Ghatafan tribes and invited them to join the Quraysh. After the Ghatafan agreed to join in, they went to other tribes, presenting them with the same plan backed by the Quraysh.

Thus an alliance was formed between the Quraysh, the Jews, and the Ghatafan against the Muslims.

Certain conditions were drawn up. The Quraysh had to gather four thousand fighters and the Ghatafan six thousand, making ten thousand in all. This vast army was to be commanded by Abu Sufyan ibn Harb. The Jews agreed to give one year's harvest of Khaybar to the Ghatafan to compensate them for their military expenses.

Wisdom is the lost property of the believer

The Muslims decided to fortify themselves in Madinah and defend the city. Their army numbered less than three thousand so Salman al-Farsi suggested that a ditch should be dug around the city for protection.

'In Persia,' Salman said, 'when we feared invaders, we would dig a ditch around us to keep them at bay.'

The Messenger of Allah agreed to his suggestion and a ditch was dug on the exposed side from where they feared the enemy would attack. The Messenger of Allah planned the work and assigned forty cubits of digging to each group of ten Muslims. The length of the ditch was about five thousand cubits and its depth varied between seven and ten cubits. Its width was at least nine cubits.

The spirit of equality and mutual support among the Muslims

The Messenger of Allah helped to dig the ditch and encouraged the Muslims working alongside him. Although it was bitterly cold and food was in short supply, the work proceeded smoothly.

Abu Talhah said, 'We complained to the Messenger of Allah of hunger and we showed him the stones that we had tied round our bellies to ease the pain. Then the Messenger of Allah showed us that he had two stones on his belly.'

In spite of all this they were happy, praising Allah and chanting poems. No one complained or expressed any regrets.

Anas (may Allah be pleased with him) said, 'The Messenger of Allah went out to the ditch when the Muhajirun and Ansar were digging in the bitterly cold morning air. They had no slaves to do it for them. Seeing their state of fatigue and hunger, he said:

> O Allah! True life is the life of the Next World.
> So forgive the Ansar and the Muhajirun.

In response they said:

> We are those who have given homage to Muhammad.
> To fight in *jihad* as long as we have life.

The Muslims came upon a large rock which their picks could not shift. When they complained to the Messenger of Allah about it, he took up a pick, saying, 'In the name of Allah.' His first blow broke off a third of the rock and sent sparks flying.

'Allah is greater!' he said. 'I have been given the keys of Syria. By Allah, I see its red castles, if Allah wills.'

He struck at the rock a second time and another third broke off.

'Allah is greater. I have been given the keys of Persia and, by Allah, I see the white castles of al-Mada'in.'

With his third blow, he invoked the name of Allah and the rest of the rock shattered.

'Allah is greater!' he exclaimed, 'Allah is greater! I have been given the keys of the Yemen. By Allah, I see the gates of San'a' from here.'

Prophetic miracles

A number of miracles were witnessed by the Companions at this time. Once when the ground was too hard to dig in part of the ditch, the Messenger of Allah called for some water, spat into it and prayed a supplication willed by Allah. When he poured the water over the hard ground, it became soft like sand. On other occasions, a great blessing would appear when a small amount of food could satisfy a large number of Muslims or even be sufficient for an entire army of three thousand workers.

'When they came to you from above you and from beneath you'

The Muslims had scarcely finished work on the ditch when the Quraysh and the Ghatafan arrived and pitched camp outside Madinah with ten thousand warriors. The Messenger of Allah assembled his three thousand Muslims, keeping the ditch between them and the enemy.

A treaty existed between the Muslims and the Madinan Jewish tribe of Banu Qurayzah. Huyayy ibn Akhtab, the chief of Banu'n-Nadir encouraged the Jews to break the treaty. When the Messenger of Allah heard of this, he realized that it was a serious setback and everyone feared the consequences. Some of the hypocrites displayed their hypocrisy openly. The Messenger of Allah even considered making a treaty with the Ghatafan, giving them one-third of Madinah's dates in order to make things easier for the Ansar who always bore the greatest hardships during wars.

He rejected that option after Sa'd ibn Mu'adh and Sa'd ibn 'Ubadah advised him to remain firm, upright and resolute before the enemy and to refuse any compromise.

'Messenger of Allah,' they said, 'We and these people all used to associate other things with Allah and worship idols; none of us worshipped nor recognized Allah. They would not eat a single date except through hospitality or purchase. Now that Allah has honoured us with Islam and guided us to it and made us mighty by you and Himself, shall we still give them our property? By Allah, we have no need to and, by Allah, we will not give them anything but the sword until Allah decides between us and them.'

Quraysh cavalry

The Messenger of Allah and the Muslims remained besieged by their enemies but no fighting took place. However, some of the mounted Quraysh galloped their horses up to the edge of the ditch. When they saw the ditch, they said, 'By Allah, this is a device which the Arabs have never used!'

Then, having found the narrowest part, they beat their horses until they jumped over the ditch into the territory of Madinah. Among them was the famous horseman 'Amr ibn 'Abd Wudd who was said to be the equal of a thousand horsemen. He stopped and asked, 'Who will face me?'

'Ali ibn Abi Talib sprang forward and said, ' 'Amr!

You swore by Allah that if a man of the Quraysh offered you two alternatives, you would accept one of them!'

'Yes, I did.'

'I call you to Allah and to His Messenger and to Islam,' 'Ali said.

'I have no need of that.'

'Then I call on you to encounter me.'

'Nephew,' said 'Amr to 'Ali, 'By Allah, I do not want to kill you.'

'But, by Allah,' 'Ali replied, 'I want to kill you.'

'Amr was so furious that he leapt from his horse, hamstrung it, and slapped its face. Then he advanced on 'Ali who fought back. They circled one another, thrusting and parrying. 'Ali (may Allah be pleased with him) eventually beheaded 'Amr with a sweeping blow of his sword. The other horsemen rapidly retreated back across the ditch.

A mother encouraging her son to fight and gain martyrdom

Before the veil was prescribed, 'A'ishah, *Umm al-Mu'minin,* said that she was with the Muslim women in the fortress of Banu Harithah when, 'Sa'd ibn Mu'adh passed by wearing armour so short that his forearm was exposed. He was chanting some verses and his mother called, "Catch up, my son. By Allah, you are late." '

'A'ishah continued, 'I said to her, "Umm Sa'd, I wish Sa'd's armour were longer than that." '

What 'A'ishah feared took place. Sa'd ibn Mu'adh was hit by an arrow which severed a vein causing excessive bleeding. He died a martyr in the subsequent battle with the Banu Qurayzah.

To Allah belong the armies of the heavens and the earth

Their enemies laid siege to the Muslims for about a month. They invaded all the surrounding areas creating great hardship. The hypocrites showed their true colours; some even asked the Messenger of Allah if they could go into Madinah because they had left their houses unlocked. In reality, they only wanted to flee from the battlefront.

While the Messenger of Allah and his Companions kept a close watch on the enemy besieging them, Nu'aym ibn Mas'ud from the Ghatafan came up to him to say, 'Messenger of Allah, I have become a Muslim but my people do not know that. Tell me what you want me to do and I will do whatever you wish.'

The Messenger of Allah replied, 'You are the only Muslim there, so stay among our enemies and try to help us in whatever way you can. War is a clever device.'

Nu'aym ibn Mas'ud then went to the Banu Quray-zah and aroused doubts in their minds about their position. He mentioned their alliance with the Quraysh and Ghatafan who were distant tribes, and their antagonism towards the Muhajirun and Ansar who were their close neighbours. He suggested they should not fight alongside the Quraysh and Ghatafan until they had taken some leaders as hostages for security. They answered, 'You have given us good advice.'

When he went to talk to the Quraysh, he told them that the Jews were regretting what they had done and would be asking for some of their leaders to be held hostage as security that the treaty would not be broken. He also said that when they handed them over to the Prophet and his Companions, they would strike off their heads. Then he told the Ghatafan the same story as he had told the Quraysh. The seeds of distrust that he planted in their minds put the two groups on their guard and made them angry with the Jews. A split developed between the allies as a result, and each of them feared the others.

When Abu Sufyan and the leaders of the Ghatafan were ready to fight a decisive battle with the Muslims, the Jews put it off, demanding hostages from both sides first. The Quraysh and Ghatafan were convinced that Nu'aym ibn Mas'ud had told them the truth so they refused to grant the Jews' request. The Jews were also convinced that he had told them the truth. Thus their distrust of each other broke their unity and they split up.

Allah supported His Messenger by causing a hurricane to blow during the cold wintry nights. It blew down the enemy's tents and overturned their cooking-pots. The men were disheartened. Abu Sufyan got up and said,

'Company of Quraysh! By Allah, we are not in a permanent camp. The horses and camels are dying. The Banu Qurayzah have broken their promise to us and we have heard things about them which we dislike. We have suffered from the harshness of the wind as you can see and we are left without a cooking pot, or a fire. Not even a tent is standing up. Leave now, for I am going.'

Abu Sufyan went to his camel which was hobbled and mounted it. He beat it but did not unhobble it until it was standing.

When the Ghatafan heard that the Quraysh had departed, they also left. The Messenger of Allah was standing in prayer when his spy, Hudhayfah ibn al-Yaman, informed him of what had taken place. In the morning the Messenger of Allah left the ditch and returned to Madinah.

All the Muslims followed him, laying down their weapons. Allah Almighty spoke the truth:

> *O you who believe, remember Allah's blessing on you when hosts came against you, and We loosed against them a wind, and hosts you did not see. Allah sees what you do.* (33: 9) and, *Allah sent back those that were unbelievers in their rage and they attained no good. Allah spared the believers of fighting. Surely Allah is Strong, Mighty.* (33: 25)

The hardships of war were over and the Quraysh never again returned to fight the Muslims.

The Messenger of Allah said, 'The Quraysh will never raid you after this year. Rather you will raid them.'

Seven Muslims were martyred on the Day of the Ditch while four idolworshippers were killed by the Muslims.

The Expedition Against the Banu Qurayzah

The Banu Qurayzah break a treaty

When the Messenger of Allah came to Madinah, he had a covenant drawn up between the Muhajirun and Ansar to which the Jews were also a party. The Jews were given freedom of religion and protection of life and property. They had reciprocal obligations. The clauses included: 'Each must help the other against anyone who attacks. They must seek mutual advice and consultation, and piety rather than wrongdoing. They are bound to help one another against any attack on Yathrib.'

However Huyayy ibn Akhtab, the Jew who was leader of the Banu'n-Nadir, encouraged the Banu Qurayzah to break the treaty and to collaborate with the Quraysh although another leader, Ka'b ibn Asad al-Qurazi, had said, 'I have seen nothing but truthfulness and loyalty in Muhammad.' But Ka'b ibn Asad broke his word and absolved himself of any promise made between himself and the Messenger of Allah. When this news reached the Prophet, he sent Sa'd ibn Mu'adh (may Allah be pleased with him), leader of the Aws (allies of the Banu Qurayzah) and Sa'd ibn 'Ubadah, leader of the Khazraj, with some Ansar representatives for confirmation. They found the situation even worse than they had feared.

'Who is the Messenger of Allah? There is no treaty or agreement between us and Muhammad,' the Banu Qurayzah alleged.

They were preparing to attack the Muslims, threatening to stab them in the back. That was harder to bear and more harmful than any onslaught on an open battlefield. It is referred to in the Qur'an: *'When they came against you from above you and from underneath you.'* (33: 10)

The situation was extremely perilous for the Muslims.

The advance on the Banu Qurayzah

When the Messenger of Allah and the Muslims left the ditch to return to Madinah they laid down their weapons. Jibril appeared and asked, 'Have you laid down your weapons, Messenger of Allah?'

'Yes,' he answered.

'The angels have not yet laid down their weapons. Allah the Mighty and Exalted commands you to go to the Banu Qurayzah. I am also to go there to shake them.'

The Messenger of Allah had it announced that: 'Whoever hears and obeys should not pray *'Asr* before arriving at the Banu Qurayzah.'

He pitched camp and laid siege to the Banu Qurayzah for twenty-five days. By then they were so hard pressed that they surrendered for Allah had cast terror into their hearts.

Although the Banu Qurayzah submitted to the judgement of the Messenger of Allah, the leaders of the Aws interceded on their behalf. They maintained that the Banu Qurayzah were their allies against the Khazraj. The

Messenger of Allah said, 'Will you be satisfied, Aws, if one of your men gives judgement on them?'

'Yes,' they replied.

The Messenger of Allah said, 'Sa'd ibn Mu'adh is the right man.'

When Sa'd was brought to him, the Aws people begged him, 'Abu 'Amr! Deal well with your friends. The Messenger of Allah appointed you for that so that you could be good to them.'

When they persisted, he said, 'A time has come when Sa'd is beyond caring about the praise or blame of anyone. I judge that the men be killed and their property divided up and that their children and women be taken as slaves.'

The Messenger of Allah said, 'You have given the judgement of Allah regarding them.'

The judgement conformed with the law of war laid down for the Children of Isra'il given in the Torah. Sa'd ibn Mu'adh's sentence was carried out on the Banu Qurayzah and the Muslims were made safe from any acts of treachery.

Sallam ibn Abi'l-Huqayq was one of the Jews who had formed the confederation against the Muslims. The Khazraj killed him at his house in Khaybar. The Aws had already killed Ka'b ibn al-Ashraf who had done his utmost to incite the Quraysh against the Muslims and to slander the Messenger of Allah. Thus, the Muslims were saved from the leaders of enemy movements against Islam.

Thumamah ibn Uthal

The Messenger of Allah sent mounted soldiers towards Najd. They captured Thumamah ibn Uthal, the chief of the Banu Hanifah. When they returned to Madinah, they tied him to one of the columns of the Messenger of Allah's mosque.

The Messenger of Allah passed by him and said, 'What do you expect, Thumamah?'

He answered, 'Muhammad! If you kill me, you kill someone whose blood must be avenged. If you are gracious, you are gracious to someone who will be grateful. If you want money, ask what you like and it will be given!' The Messenger of Allah left him. When he passed by him again he asked the same question and received the same reply. On the third occasion he said, 'Release Thumamah,' so they set him free.

Thumamah went to a palm grove near the mosque where he washed himself. He returned to the mosque and became a Muslim, declaring, 'By Allah, there was no one on the face of the earth whose face was more detested by me than yours. Now your face has become the dearest of faces to me. By Allah, there was no religion on the face of the earth more hateful to me than yours and now it is the dearest of all to me. Your cavalry seized me when I was going to perform *'umrah.'*

The Messenger of Allah congratulated him and invited him to perform *'umrah.*

When Thumamah came to Makkah, the Quraysh said, 'Have you left your religion, Thumamah?'

'No, by Allah, but I have become a Muslim with Muhammad. No, by Allah, not a grain of wheat will come to you from Yamamah until the Messenger of Allah gives permission for it.' Yamamah had extremely fertile land and was the main supplier of grain to Makkah.

Thumamah went back home and forbade any caravans from transporting goods to Makkah. The Quraysh became so desperate that they wrote to the Messenger of Allah asking him, because of their kinship, to write to Thumamah to get the food ban lifted. The Messenger of Allah (may Allah bless him and grant him peace) did just that, and grain was once again brought to Makkah.

We have granted you a manifest victory (Qurān 48:1).

The Peace Treaty of Hudaybiyyah

The Messenger of Allah's dream

The Messenger of Allah dreamt that he entered Makkah and did *tawaf* around the Ka'bah. His Companions in Madinah were delighted when he told them about it. They all revered Makkah and the Ka'bah and they yearned to do *tawaf* there.

The Muhajirun had even greater affection for Makkah. They had been born there and had grown up in the city. They loved it deeply but had been driven away from it. When the Messenger of Allah told them of his dream, they started to prepare for the journey to Makkah. Hardly anyone wanted to stay behind.

Makkah visited at last

The Messenger of Allah left Madinah for al-Hudaybiyyah in Dhu'l-Qa'dah, 6 A.H. He intended to perform *'umrah* in peace. He was accompanied by fifteen hundred Muslims dressed as pilgrims for *'umrah* in order to show people that they had come to visit the Ka'bah out of respect for it. They took with them animals for the sacrifice.

The Messenger of Allah sent out a scout in advance

to inform him about the reaction of the Quraysh. When he was near 'Usfan the scout returned and reported, 'I left Ka'b ibn Lu'ayy gathering an army against you to prevent you from reaching the Ka'bah.'

The Messenger of Allah continued to travel until he reached the furthest part of al-Hudaybiyyah. He pitched camp although there was little water. The people started to complain to him of thirst. He took an arrow from his quiver and told them to put it in the waterhole. Immediately it began to gush with water and continued to flow until they had all quenched their thirst.

The Quraysh were extremely alarmed when they heard that the Muslims were at al-Hudaybiyyah. The Messenger of Allah decided to send one of his Companions to them and summoned 'Uthman ibn 'Affan. He was sent to inform the Quraysh that they had not come to fight but had come for *'umrah,* and that he should call them to Islam. The Messenger of Allah instructed him to visit the believing men and women of Makkah, to give them the good news of victory and tell them that Allah, the Mighty and Exalted, would make His religion victorious in Makkah and it would no longer be necessary for them to conceal their belief.

'Uthman went to Makkah and conveyed the message to Abu Sufyan and the Quraysh noblemen.

When 'Uthman had finished delivering the message, they said, 'If you yourself wish to do *tawaf* of the House, go ahead.'

'I will not do it,' he said, 'until the Messenger of Allah has done *tawaf.*'

Bay'at-ar-Ridwan

'Uthman was in Makkah longer than the Muslims

had expected and the rumour spread that he had been killed. Then the Messenger of Allah called for a pledge of allegiance. He sat beneath a tree and the Muslims promised that they would fight with him to the last man. The Messenger of Allah took his own hand and said, 'This is for 'Uthman.' Later they heard that 'Uthman had not been murdered and he came back safely.

The Pledge took place under an acacia tree in al-Hudaybiyyah and is referred to in the Qur'an. Allah revealed, *'Allah was pleased with the believers when they were pledging their allegiance under the tree.'* (48: 18)

The deadlock between the Quraysh and the Muslims continued until four envoys came to the Messenger of Allah who said to each one, 'We did not come to fight anyone. Rather we came to perform *'umrah.'*

But the Quraysh remained stubborn and refused to allow them to proceed.

One of the envoys, 'Urwah ibn Mas'ud ath-Thaqafi, went back to his people and said, 'O people! By Allah, I have been in the presence of kings – from Chosroes, and Caesar to the Negus – and by Allah, I have never seen any king whose people respected him as much as the companions of Muhammad respect Muhammad.' He described to them what he had seen.

Treaty and truce; wisdom and forbearance

The Quraysh then sent Suhayl ibn 'Amr. When the Messenger of Allah saw him coming, he remarked, 'It is clear that they want peace since they have sent this man.' He told his Companions to prepare a draft agreement.

He called for 'Ali ibn Abi Talib and told him, 'Write: In the name of Allah, the Merciful, the Compassionate.'

'By Allah,' Suhayl said, 'we do not know who this "Merciful" is. Rather write, "In Your name, O Allah" as you used to write.'

The Muslims said, 'By Allah, we will only write, "In the name of Allah, the Merciful, the Compassionate."'

The Prophet said, 'Write, "In Your name, O Allah."'

Then he said, 'Write, "This is what Muhammad, the Messenger of Allah has agreed."'

'By Allah,' retorted Suhayl, 'if we accepted that you were the Messenger of Allah, we would not have prevented you from reaching the House of Allah nor fought you. Rather write, "Muhammad ibn 'Abdullah."'

The Prophet said, 'I am the Messenger of Allah even though you do not believe me. Write, "Muhammad ibn 'Abdullah."'

He asked 'Ali to erase what he had written but 'Ali said, 'By Allah no, I will not erase it.'

The Messenger of Allah said, 'Show me the place,' and he erased it himself. Then he said, 'This is what the Messenger of Allah agrees provided that you give us leave to perform *tawaf* of the Ka'bah.'

Suhayl said, 'By Allah, we will not allow the Arabs to say that we submitted to pressure. It will have to be next year.' It was also written: 'On the condition that if any of our men, even if he has your religion, comes to you, you will return him to us.'

The Muslims said, 'Glory be to Allah! How can we return someone to the idolworshippers after he has become a Muslim?'

While they were thus engaged, Abu Jandal ibn Suhayl came on the scene fettered by chains. He had escaped from Makkah, and threw himself down among the Muslims.

Suhayl looked at his son and commented, 'Muhammad, here is the first man that you have to return under this treaty.'

'We have not finished the document yet,' countered the Prophet.

'Then, by Allah, I will never agree to anything.'

'Let me keep him,' said the Messenger of Allah.

'I will not allow you to keep him.'

'Let him go for my sake.'

'I will not.'

'O Muslims!' said Abu Jandal, 'Am I to be returned to the idolworshippers when I have come to you as a Muslim? Do you not see what I have suffered?' He had been severely tortured for his beliefs. However, the Prophet returned him as his father had demanded.

The two parties agreed to abandon war for ten years. During that period everyone would live in peace. Both sides would be safe and would refrain from fighting one another. Whoever came to Muhammad (may Allah bless him and grant him peace) from the Quraysh without obtaining the permission of his guardian would be returned to them, but whoever came to the Quraysh from those with Muhammad need not be returned to him. Whoever wanted to enter into an alliance and agreement with Muhammad could do so and whoever wanted to enter into an alliance and agreement with the Quraysh would also be free to do so.

The Muslims' distress

When the Muslims saw the terms of the truce and what it meant to the Messenger of Allah, they were very distressed. The effect on them was so great that 'Umar ibn al-Khattab asked Abu Bakr angrily, 'Did not the Messenger of Allah say to us that we were going to go to the Ka'bah and perform *tawaf*?'

'Yes. But did he tell you that it was going to be this very year?'

'No.'

Abu Bakr assured him, 'You will go there and you will do *tawaf*.'

When the Messenger of Allah had finished drawing up the treaty, he sacrificed a camel and then shaved his head. This was a difficult time for the Muslims because all their hopes had been dashed. They had left Madinah with the firm intention of entering Makkah and doing *'umrah*. Now they felt beaten and crushed. However, when they saw that the Messenger of Allah had made the sacrifice and shaved his head, they rushed to follow his example.

A humiliating peace or a clear victory?

Then the Messenger of Allah broke camp and returned to Madinah. On his journey back, Allah confirmed that the truce of Hudaybiyyah was not a set-back but a victory:

> *Surely We have given you a clear victory, that Allah may forgive you your former and later sins, and complete His blessing on you and guide you on a straight path and that Allah may help you with a mighty help.* (48: 1–3)

'Umar (may Allah be pleased with him) said, 'Is this a victory then, Messenger of Allah?'

He replied, 'Yes.'

Outcome of the treaty

Not long after the Messenger of Allah had returned to Madinah, a man named Abu Basir 'Utbah ibn Usayd came from Makkah to join the Muslims. The Quraysh sent emissaries to fetch him back. They said, 'Under the terms of the treaty which you made with us you must hand him over.' So the Messenger of Allah allowed them to take Abu Basir with them. But on the way back to Makkah, he escaped from them and fled to the coast. Abu Jandal ibn Suhayl also escaped and joined Abu Basir. Then everyone who had become a Muslim and who had suffered persecution from the Quraysh joined Abu Basir until they comprised a group numbering seventy. They set themselves up on a trade route. Whenever they heard that a caravan of the Quraysh had left for Syria, they waylaid it, killed the merchants and took the goods they were carrying.

The Hudaybiyyah treaty gave the idolworshippers and Muslims an opportunity to mix. The idolworshippers soon came to appreciate the good qualities of the Muslims. Before a year had passed, many of them had become Muslims, and the Quraysh leaders were worried about their influence.

They sent to the Prophet, begging him by Allah and by kinship, not to return the men to Makkah but to keep them in Madinah. From then on whoever of them came to him from Makkah was safe.

These moves indicated that the Treaty of al-Hudaybiyyah in which the Messenger of Allah had accepted all the Quraysh conditions had been beneficial after all. The treaty had been a decisive step in gaining further victories for Islam and in spreading the faith throughout the Arabian peninsula with great speed. It led to the conquest of Makkah and the opportunity to invite the kings of the world – Caesar, Chosroes, Muqawqis and the Arabian princes – to accept Islam. Allah the Great revealed:

> *Yet it may happen that you will hate a thing which is better for you; and it may happen that you will love a thing which is worse for you. Allah knows, and you know not.* (2: 216)

Khalid ibn al-Walid and 'Amr ibn al-'As accept Islam

Khalid ibn al-Walid, general of the Quraysh cavalry and the hero of great battles, was among those who accepted Islam. The Messenger of Allah called him the 'Sword of Allah'. He fought bravely in the way of Allah and was the conqueror of Syria. 'Amr ibn al-'As, another great commander and subsequently the conqueror of Egypt, also became a Muslim. Both of these strong leaders came to Madinah after the Treaty of al-Hudaybiyyah.

Inviting the Kings and Rulers to Islam

An invitation

Peaceful conditions followed the treaty of Hudaybiyyah and the Messenger of Allah wrote letters to foreign sovereigns and to Arab chieftains, inviting them to accept Islam. He took great care to select a suitable messenger for each king and the letters were painstakingly prepared. He was told that foreign kings would not accept any letter without a seal so he had a silver signet ring made on which was inscribed, 'Muhammad, Messenger of Allah.'

Heraclius

Among the kings he contacted were the Byzantine emperor, Heraclius, the Persian emperor, Chosroes Parvez, the Negus, King of Abyssinia, and Muqawqis, King of Egypt.

Heraclius, the Negus and Muqawqis received their letters with respect and gave courteous replies. Heraclius wanted to know more about the Prophet and dispatched men to find out all they could. Abu Sufyan happened to be in Ghazzah on a business trip and he was presented to the king. Heraclius proved to be an intelligent examiner who knew the history of religion and the qualities and behaviour

THE PROPHET'S DELEGATES TO NEIGHBOURING SOVEREIGNS

1 Hātib ibn Abū Balta'ah to Muqauqis, Alexandria.
2 Daḥyah al Kalbī to Heraclius, Jerusalem.
3 Shujā' ibn Wahb al Asadī to al-Ḥārith al-Ghassānī, Damascus.
4 'Abdullah ibn Hudhāfah al Sahmī to Chosroes, Madā'in, (Ctesiphon).
5 'Alā' ibn al Ḥaḍramī to Al Mundhir ibn Sāwa, Baḥrayn.
6 Sulayṭ ibn 'Amr al 'Āmirī to Hawdhah ibn 'Alī, Yamāmah.
7 'Amr ibn al 'Āṣ to Jayfar al Jalandī, 'Umān.
8 'Amr ibn Umayyah al Ḍimrī to the Negus, Abyssinia.

of the Prophets. He had studied how nations reacted to them and how and when Allah would send them. Abu Sufyan was truthful in his answers in the tradition of the early Arabs who considered it beneath their dignity to tell a lie.

When Heraclius heard Abu Sufyan's answers, he was certain that Muhammad was the Prophet of Allah. He said, 'If what you say is true, he will come to possess the place on which my two feet are standing. I knew that one was due to come forth but I did not think that he would come from you. If I knew that I could reach him, I would set out to meet him. If I was with him, I would wash his feet.'

He summoned the Roman generals to the castle and commanded that the doors be shut. Then he went to them, declaring, 'O Romans! If you want success and right guidance and to establish and strengthen your kingdom, give homage to this Prophet.'

They disliked what he was saying and tried to leave but they found that the doors were locked. When Heraclius saw their reaction, he despaired of their faith. He said, 'Return those people to me,' and to them he repeated, 'What I said before was to test your faith. Now I have seen it.'

They prostrated before him and were pleased with what he had said.

Heraclius had preferred his kingdom to Islam. Wars and battles continued between him and the Muslims during the caliphate of Abu Bakr and 'Umar when he lost both his kingdom and his power.

The Negus and Muqawqis

The Negus and the Muqawqis were most courteous to the envoys sent by the Messenger of Allah. The

Muqawqis sent him gifts, including two slavegirls. One of them was Mariah, the mother of Ibrahim, the son of the Messenger of Allah.

Chosroes

When Chosroes, the emperor of Persia, read the letter, he tore it up indignantly, 'How dare this person who is my slave write to me like this!' he demanded.

When the Messenger of Allah heard about Chosroes' reaction, he replied, 'Allah will shatter his kingdom.'

Chosroes commanded Badhan, his governor in Yemen, to bring the Messenger of Allah to him. Badhan delegated the task to Babawayh. When Babawayh came to the Messenger of Allah in Madinah, he said, 'The King of Kings, Chosroes, wrote to King Badhan commanding him to send out men to bring you to him. He has sent me to fetch you.'

However, the Messenger of Allah told him that Allah had given Shirawayh power and he would kill his father Chosroes. And indeed that was the truth. Allah shattered the Sassanid kingdom which had existed for four hundred years, and gave the Muslims power over it. He guided the Persian people to Islam.

The Expedition to Khaybar

Reward from Allah

Allah – glory be to Him and may He be exalted! – promised those who had made the Pledge at Hudaybiyyah the reward of coming victory as well as booty. The Qur'an says:

> *Allah was well pleased with the believers when they were pledging allegiance to you under the tree, and He knew what was in their hearts, so He sent down Tranquillity upon them, and rewarded them with a near victory and many spoils to take; and Allah is ever Mighty, Wise.* (48: 18–19)

The Conquest of Khaybar was to be the first of these victories. Khaybar, seventy miles northeast of Madinah, was a Jewish colony with citadels and was the headquarters of the Jewish garrison. It was the last and most formidable Jewish stronghold in Arabia. The Messenger of Allah wanted to be secure on that front because the Jews spent much of their wealth on stirring up the neighbouring Arab tribes to wage war against the Muslims.

THE CONQUEST OF KHAYBAR (MUHARRAM 7 A.H.)

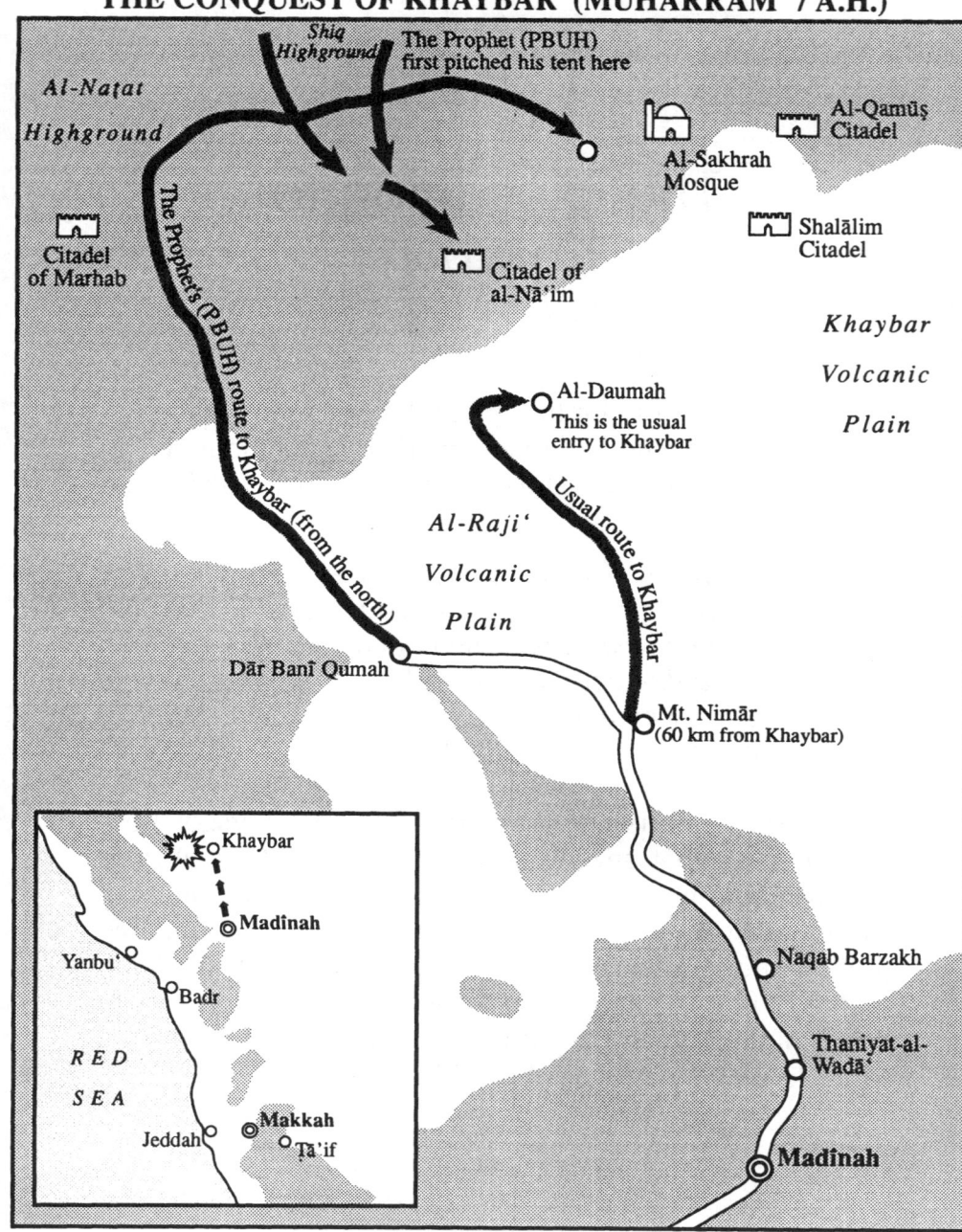

An army of believers

On his return from al-Hudaybiyyah, the Messenger of Allah stayed in Madinah during the month of Dhu'l-Hijjah and for part of Muharram. At the end of Muharram, he set out for Khaybar. While travelling, one of the Companions, 'Amir ibn al-Akwa' recited these verses:

> By Allah, were it not for Allah, we would not
> have been guided nor given *sadaqah*, charity,
> nor prayed.
> If people treat us unjustly
> or try to attack us we resist.
> Send down tranquillity
> and make us firm against the enemy.

The Messenger of Allah advanced with his army which numbered fourteen hundred men including two hundred cavalry. Those who had lagged behind on the al-Hudaybiyyah expedition were refused permission to take part in the expedition. Twenty women accompanied the party in order to care for the sick and wounded and to prepare food and supply water during the fighting.

On the way, the Messenger of Allah called for food but only some dried up barley was brought. He asked for it to be moistened, then he and all those who accompanied him ate it. When he was approaching Khaybar, the Messenger of Allah prayed for the benefits that would come from conquering the colony and sought refuge from its evil and the evil of its people. When he went on an expedition against a people, he would not attack until morning. When, if he heard the *adhan* from the locality, he held back, it was a sign that there were believers among the inhabitants. But if he did not hear the *adhan,* he would attack. The *adhan* was not heard the next morning so the army advanced. They met the early workers of Khaybar carrying their spades and baskets but when they saw the Messenger of Allah and the army, they cried, 'Muhammad with his army!' and fled. The Messenger of Allah said, 'Allah is great! Khaybar is destroyed! When we arrive in a community, it is a bad morning for those who have been warned.'

A victorious general

The Messenger of Allah and his army overpowered the fortresses of Khaybar one by one. The first fortress to be conquered was that of Na'im. The Jews defended well against the Muslims but 'Ali ibn Abi Talib eventually crushed them. The Messenger of Allah had said, 'Let the standard be taken by a man who loves Allah and His Messenger and he will conquer this fort.'

All the great Companions (may Allah be pleased with them) vied for this honour, as each of them hoped to be the standard-bearer. The Messenger of Allah called 'Ali ibn Abi Talib, whose eyes were inflamed, to him and he applied spittle to his eyes while praying for his success. 'Ali's eyes were soon cured and he received the standard. He said, 'I will fight them until they are like us.'

The Messenger of Allah replied, 'Go ahead and invite them to Islam. Tell them the obligations they owe to Allah. By Allah, if one man is guided to the faith by you it is better for you than having red camels.'

Another victory

When 'Ali came near the fort, Marhab, the famous Jewish war-lord, appeared reciting verses about his bravery.

They fell upon one another immediately. 'Ali's sword ran through Marhab's helmet, splitting his head in two. A great victory was gained through his death.

The slave's reward

A black Abyssinian slave was tending sheep for his Jewish master when he saw the Jews taking up arms. He was told that they were going to fight the man who claimed to be a Prophet. The slave was curious. He took his sheep right up to the Messenger of Allah and asked, 'What is it that you say, and what do you invite people to?'

'I invite people to Islam; that is, you testify that there is no god but Allah, that I am the Messenger of Allah and that you worship only Allah.'

'What will I get if I testify and believe in Allah?'

'You will enter Paradise if you die with this faith.'

The slave accepted Islam and then asked, 'Prophet of Allah! I hold these sheep in trust. What should I do with the flock?'

The Messenger of Allah replied, 'Abandon them in the field near the fort. Allah will make sure that they reach their master.'

The slave did as he was told and the sheep returned to their master. The Jew then discovered that his slave had become a Muslim. The Messenger of Allah urged his people to fight for the sake of Allah. When the battle between the Muslims and Jews was under way, the black slave was among the Muslims who were fighting and were martyred. The Messenger of Allah came to his Companions to say, 'Allah has blessed this slave and brought him to Khaybar. I saw two *houris* by him even though he had never prostrated to Allah.'

The Bedouin's reward

A Bedouin also came to the Messenger of Allah and accepted Islam. He then went to accompany the Messenger of Allah in the campaign. Some of the Companions were asked to take care of him.

When, on the expedition to Khaybar, the Messenger of Allah captured some booty, he allocated a share to the Bedouin who was some distance away grazing the Muslims' flocks. When he came and was given his booty, he asked, 'What is this?'

'A share which the Messenger of Allah has allotted to you.'

He then took it to the Prophet and asked, 'What is this, Messenger of Allah?'

'A portion of the booty which I have allotted to you.'

'I did not follow you for this,' he said. 'I followed you so that I might be shot with an arrow here,' and he pointed to his neck, 'and die and enter Paradise.'

'If that is what you want,' the Prophet told him, 'Allah will confirm it.'

In a later battle the Bedouin's dead body was brought to the Messenger of Allah.

'Is it the same man?' he asked.

'Yes.'

'He was true to Allah and Allah made his wish come true,' said the Messenger of Allah who shrouded him with his own cloak. Then he recited the funeral prayer over him. His words included, 'O Allah, this is Your slave who went out as a *muhajir* in Your way. He was killed as a martyr and I am a witness for him.'

Conditions for remaining in Khaybar

The Jews of Khaybar were besieged in their fortresses. Fighting continued for days. At last they asked the Messenger of Allah for terms of peace. He allowed them to stay in Khaybar on condition that they gave to the Muslims in Madinah half of all the crops and fruit they produced on their farms. Each year the Messenger of Allah used to send 'Abdullah ibn Rawahah to Khaybar where he divided the produce in half and let the Jews choose the half they wanted. 'On this the heavens and earth stand' was the Jews' comment on his sense of justice.

Poisoned meat

During the Khaybar expedition, an attempt was made to poison the Messenger of Allah. A Jewess, Zaynab bint al-Harith, the wife of Sallam ibn Mishkam, presented him with roasted mutton, having enquired what joint he liked best. When she was told, 'shoulder,' she put a quantity of poison in it and took it to him. When he tasted it, he realized immediately that it was poisoned and spat it out.

He summoned the Jews who gathered round and asked them, 'Will you be truthful about something I will ask of you?'

They said, 'Yes.'

'Did you put poison in this mutton?'

'Yes.'

'What made you do it?'

'If you were false,' they said, 'we would get rid of you. But if you are really a Prophet, the poison would not harm you.'

Zaynab was then brought to the Messenger of Allah. She confessed, 'I wanted to kill you.'

He answered, 'Allah would not give you power over me.'

His Companions asked, 'Shall we kill her?'

'No,' he said, and she was set free.

However, when Bishr ibn al-Bara' ibn Ma'rur, who had also eaten some of the mutton, died a painful death, Zaynab was killed.

Booty

After the Messenger of Allah had conquered Khaybar, he went on to Fadak and then to Wadi'l-Qura. He invited the Jews to Islam, telling them that if they became Muslims, their life and property would be safe and they would be rewarded by Allah. The Jews of Wadi'l-Qura decided to fight the Muslims but were soon forced to surrender.

The Jews handed over their possessions and the Muslims took them as booty. The Messenger of Allah then divided things up between his Companions, leaving the land and property in the Jews' hands.

When the Jews of Tayma' learnt that the Messenger of Allah had defeated the people of Khaybar, Fadak and Wadi'l-Qura, they offered him peace terms which he accepted. They were allowed to keep their land and property. The Messenger of Allah then returned to Madinah.

'Umrat al-Qada'

In the following year, 7 A.H., the Messenger of

Allah and the Muslims set out for Makkah. The Quraysh of Makkah vacated their houses and stayed up in the mountains overlooking the valley. The Muslims stayed in Makkah for three days and performed *'umrah*. The Qur'an says:

> *Allah has indeed fulfilled the vision He vouchsafed to His Messenger truly, 'You shall enter the Holy Mosque, if Allah wills, in security, your heads shaved, your hair cut short, not fearing.' He knew what you knew not, and appointed before that a nigh victory.* (48: 27)

Rivalry

Islam changed dramatically the hearts and minds of the new Muslims. Baby daughters, who had been buried alive in the days of the *Jahiliyyah,* were now precious arrivals whose custody and upbringing were considered honourable.

When the Prophet left Makkah after *'umrah,* Umamah, the little daughter of Hamzah, followed him, calling out, 'Uncle! Uncle!'

'Ali took her hand and said to Fatimah, 'Here is your niece,' and Fatimah took care of her.

'Ali, Zayd and Ja'far all claimed her guardianship.

'Ali said, 'I will take her. She is my uncle's daughter.'

Ja'far said, 'She is my uncle's daughter too, and her aunt is my wife.'

Zayd said, 'She is my brother's daughter.'

The Messenger of Allah dealt with the controversy. He gave her to her aunt, saying, 'A maternal aunt is like a mother.'

To comfort 'Ali, he said, 'You are mine and I am yours.'

And to Ja'far he said, 'You are like me in character and appearance.'

He said to Zayd, 'You are my brother and my *mawla*.'

The Expedition to Mu'tah

An assassination

The Messenger of Allah sent al-Harith ibn 'Umayr al-Azdi with a letter to Shurahbil ibn 'Amr al-Ghassani, provincial governor of Busra, under the Byzantine emperor, Heraclius. Shurahbil ordered that al-Harith be bound and then he had him beheaded. It was unknown for a king or a prince to have an ambassador or envoy put to death. Immense danger would face envoys and ambassadors in the future if Shurahbil was allowed to get away with his action. It also humiliated the sender of the message itself. This man who had exceeded the limits had to be punished.

Repercussions

When the Messenger of Allah heard what had happened, he decided to send a military force to Busra. It was in Jumada al-'Ula in 8 A.H. when three thousand men under Zayd ibn Harithah left Madinah. The Messenger of Allah had appointed Zayd, his freed slave, as their commander and the army contained many of the leading Muhajirun and Ansar.

The Prophet said, 'If Zayd falls, then Ja'far ibn Abi

Talib is in charge. If Ja'far falls, then 'Abdullah ibn Rawahah will take over.'

The Muslims bade the soldiers a fond farewell. A long and arduous journey faced them as well as an enemy backed by the strongest empire of the world.

The Muslims advanced to Ma'an where they heard that Heraclius was at al-Balqa' with a hundred thousand Roman troops and an equally strong force drawn from Arab tribes. The Muslims camped at Ma'an for two days while deciding what to do.

Then they said, 'Let us write to the Messenger of Allah to inform him about the strength of the enemy. Either he will send us reinforcements or he will command us to go ahead and we will obey his order.'

However, 'Abdullah ibn Rawahah made a speech of encouragement. 'People! By Allah! You are reluctant to go towards the very thing you came out to search for – martyrdom. We are not fighting the enemy on the strength of numbers nor of our power. We will fight them with the religion Allah has honoured us with. Come on! We will win either way, be it victory or martyrdom.' So they set off again to face their enemy.

Dedicated fighters

When they were on the outskirts of al-Balqa', the Roman and Arab forces advanced towards them. As the enemy drew nearer the Muslims took up positions in a village called Mu'tah and this was where the battle was fought.

Zayd ibn Harithah (may Allah be pleased with him) who carried the standard of the Messenger of Allah, fought bravely until he was martyred. Then thirty-three-year-old

Ja'far took the standard and fought until he was hemmed in by the enemy. He jumped off his horse, hamstrung it and fought on foot until his right hand was sliced off. He took up the standard in his left hand but that too was cut off. He then bore the standard between his arms but eventually he fell down dead. He had received ninety wounds on his chest, shoulders and arms from spears and swords, but no injuries were found on his back.

After Ja'far was killed, 'Abdullah ibn Rawahah held the standard aloft. He got off his horse and advanced on foot. His cousin came up to him with a meat-bone saying, 'Strengthen yourself with this. You have had nothing to eat during these battles of yours.' He took the bone, ate only a little and then threw it away. He picked up his sword again and fought bravely until he was killed.

Khalid, a wise general

The Muslims agreed that Khalid ibn al-Walid (may Allah be pleased with him) should take up the standard. He was a wise and courageous leader, famous for his knowledge of military tactics. He withdrew the Muslim army southwards while the enemy withdrew to the north. Night fell. He thought it best to avoid confrontation and any further fighting in the dark. Both forces, tired from fighting, chose the safe option. The Romans had heard of Khalid's technical skills and decided not to pursue the Muslim army. They were so disheartened that they did not resume the fighting the next day and the Muslims were spared.

Advance information

While the Muslims were fighting at Mu'tah, the

Messenger of Allah described the battle scene to his Companions in Madinah. Anas ibn Malik said that he announced the death of Zayd, Ja'far and Ibn Rawahah to them before he had received the news. He said, 'Zayd took the standard and fell. Then Ja'far took it and fell. Then Ibn Rawahah took it and fell.'

The tears were trickling down his face as he spoke. He added, 'The standard was taken by one of the swords of Allah (meaning Khalid) until Allah gave the Muslims their victory.'

He also said that Allah gave Ja'far two wings in place of the two hands he had lost. With them he could fly in the Garden of Paradise wherever he wished. Thereafter he was called 'Ja'far at-Tayyar (the Great Flier'), or *Dhu'l-janahayn* ('The One with Two Wings').

Come-agains not runaways

When the returning army was near Madinah, the Messenger of Allah and the Muslims went out to meet them. It was the first time a Muslim army had returned without winning a decisive victory. Some people started to throw dust on the soldiers, shouting, 'You runaways! You fled from the path of Allah!' But the Messenger of Allah told the people, 'They are not runaways, but come-agains. They will come again to battle if Allah wills.'

The Conquest of Makkah

Preparations

When Islam was well-established in the hearts of the Muslims, Allah decided that the time had come for His Messenger and his community to enter Makkah. They would purify the Ka'bah so that it would be a blessed place of guidance for the whole world. They would restore Makkah to its previous status and the sacred city would offer security for all people once again.

A broken treaty

In the Peace Treaty of Hudaybiyyah it was laid down that anyone who wanted to enter into a treaty and alliance with the Messenger of Allah should be able to do so; and anyone who wanted to enter into a treaty and alliance with the Quraysh should also be allowed to do so. The Banu Bakr entered into an alliance with the Quraysh while the Banu Khuza'ah entered into one with the Messenger of Allah.

Longstanding hostility existed between the Banu Bakr and Banu Khuza'ah. The coming of Islam had put a barrier between the people as they had become engrossed in its affairs. The Peace Treaty enabled the Banu Bakr to settle an old score against the Banu Khuza'ah. One night the

THE CONQUEST OF MAKKAH (21st RAMAḌĀN 8 A.H.)

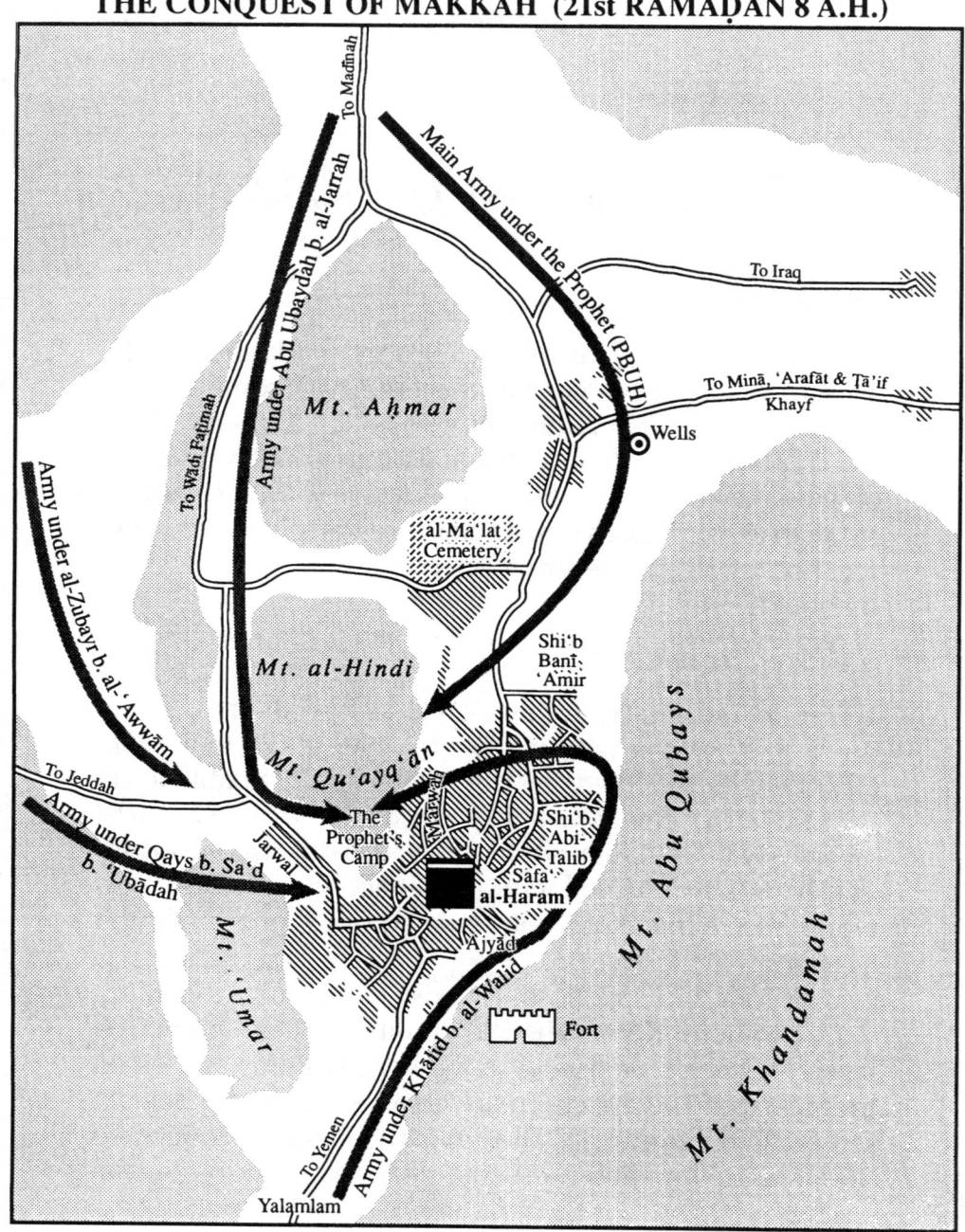

Banu Bakr attacked the Banu Khuza'ah by night when they were camped by a spring and killed some of their men. A skirmish developed and the Quraysh helped the Banu Bakr by providing weapons.

Some Quraysh leaders also fought with the Banu Bakr secretly at night, and the Khuza'ah were driven into the *Haram*. Some of the Quraysh said, 'We have entered the *Haram*. Mind your gods!' Others replied thoughtlessly, 'There is no god today, men of Banu Bakr. Take your revenge! You may never have another chance!'

Seeking help

'Amr ibn Salim al-Khuza'i went to the Messenger of Allah in Madinah and recited some verses to him about the alliance between the Muslims and the Khuza'ah. He asked for help, saying that the Quraysh had violated the agreement. His tribe had been attacked at night, he maintained, and men had been killed in *ruku'* and *sajdah*, while performing prayers.

The Messenger of Allah assured him, 'You will be helped, 'Amr ibn Salim!' He then sent a man to Makkah to get confirmation of the attack and to offer the Quraysh the chance to redress their offence. Their reply was impulsive and they ignored the likely consequences.

The Quraysh attempt to renew the treaty

When the Messenger of Allah heard their answer, he said, 'I think you will see Abu Sufyan coming to strengthen the treaty and to ask for more time.'

That happened. The Quraysh were so concerned about what they had done that they charged Abu Sufyan with the task of getting the treaty ratified.

Abu Sufyan came to the Messenger of Allah in Madinah and also went to visit his daughter, Umm Habibah, the wife of the Prophet. However, when he went to sit on the Messenger of Allah's carpet, she rolled it up from under him.

Puzzled, he said to her, 'My daughter, I do not know whether you think the carpet is too good for me or whether I am too good for the carpet.'

She replied, 'This is the Messenger of Allah's carpet and you are an unclean idolworshipper. I do not want you to sit on his carpet.'

'By Allah,' Abu Sufyan retorted. 'You have been spoiled since you left me.'

Abu Sufyan fails

Abu Sufyan went to the Messenger of Allah, but he did not receive any answer. Then he went to Abu Bakr and asked him to speak to the Messenger of Allah for him but he refused. He tried to win over 'Umar, 'Ali and Fatimah but they all said that the matter was too serious for them to get involved. Abu Sufyan became confused about what to do.

Making ready

The Messenger of Allah asked the Muslims to start preparing for an expedition but he asked them to keep it a secret. Later he announced that he was going to Makkah and ordered them to get ready.

He said, 'O Allah! Impede the informers of the Quraysh so that we can take Makkah by surprise.' He left

Madinah with ten thousand men in Ramadan 8 A.H. and advanced as far as Marr az-Zahran where they set up camp. Allah concealed this information from the Quraysh, so they waited in uncertainty.

A pardoning

On the way, the Messenger of Allah happened to meet his cousin, Abu Sufyan ibn al-Harith ibn 'Abdu'l-Muttalib. He ignored him because he had suffered insults and persecution from Abu Sufyan. The cousin complained to 'Ali that he had been ignored. 'Ali said to him, 'Go to the Messenger of Allah and say to him what the brothers said to Yusuf, *"By Allah, Allah has preferred you to us and we were indeed sinful."* (12: 91) The Messenger of Allah never likes anyone to show more mercy than he.'

Abu Sufyan ibn al-Harith did as 'Ali advised and the Messenger of Allah replied, *'Have no fear this day. Allah will forgive you. He is the Most merciful of the merciful.'*

Abu Sufyan ibn al-Harith accepted Islam and was known for his piety. He did not raise his head ever again in front of the Messenger of Allah because he felt so ashamed of his past behaviour.

Abu Sufyan ibn Harb accepts Islam

The Messenger of Allah was commanding the army and he ordered the campfires to be lit. Abu Sufyan ibn Harb, who was spying out the ground for the Quraysh, said: 'I have never seen so many fires or such an army.'

Al-'Abbas ibn 'Abdu'l-Muttalib had already left Makkah with his wife and children as a Muslim *Muhajir* and had joined the Muslim army. He recognized Abu Sufyan's voice and called to him, 'See, the Messenger of Allah is here with his army. What a terrible morning the Quraysh will have!'

He made Abu Sufyan ride on the back of his mule, fearing that if a Muslim saw him, he would kill him. Al-'Abbas took him to the Messenger of Allah who said, 'Woe to you, Abu Sufyan! Has not the time come for you to acknowledge that there is no god but Allah?'

Abu Sufyan replied, 'How kind and gentle you are! By Allah, I think that if there had been another god besides Allah, he would have helped me today.'

'Woe to you, Abu Sufyan! Is it not time that you recognized that I am the Messenger of Allah?'

Abu Sufyan replied, 'May my father and mother be your ransom! How kind and generous you are! But by Allah, I still have some doubt as to that.'

Al-'Abbas intervened, 'Woe to you, Abu Sufyan! Become a Muslim and testify that there is no god but Allah and that Muhammad is the Messenger of Allah before you lose your head.' Then Abu Sufyan recited the articles of faith and became a Muslim.

The amnesty

The Messenger of Allah was generous in granting amnesty to everyone so that no one in Makkah need be killed that morning. Only those who courted danger ran any risk of losing their life. He declared, 'Whoever enters the house of Abu Sufyan is safe. Whoever locks his door is safe. Whoever enters the mosque is safe.' The Messenger of Allah told his army not to use arms against anyone when they entered Makkah unless they met opposition or resistance.

He directed the army not to touch property or possessions belonging to the people of Makkah and nothing should be destroyed.

Abu Sufyan's influence

The Messenger of Allah decided to demonstrate the power of Islam to Abu Sufyan. He asked 'Abbas ibn 'Abdu'l-Muttalib to take Abu Sufyan to where the marching squadrons would pass by.

The Muslim squadrons passed by like a surging sea with the different tribes bearing their standards. Whenever a tribe passed by, Abu Sufyan would ask 'Abbas about it and, when he heard the name of the tribe, he would mumble gloomily, 'What have I got to do with them?' Finally the Messenger of Allah passed by with his squadron in full, gleaming green armour. It was the regiment of the Muhajirun and the Ansar. Only their eyes were visible because of their armour.

Abu Sufyan said, 'Glory be to Allah! 'Abbas, who are these?'

'This is the Messenger of Allah with the Muhajirun and Ansar,' he answered.

'No one has any power or resistance against them,' said Abu Sufyan. 'By Allah, Abu'l-Fadl, the authority of your brother's son has certainly increased.'

'Abu Sufyan,' 'Abbas said, 'This is not a kingdom, it is prophethood.'

Abu Sufyan replied, 'Then it is wonderful.'

He stood up and shouted at the top of his voice, 'O men of the Quraysh! This is Muhammad with a force you cannot resist. He has ten thousand men of steel. He says that whoever enters my house will be safe.'

The men shouted back, 'Allah slay you! What good is your house to us?'

Abu Sufyan added, 'And whoever locks himself indoors is safe and whoever enters the mosque is safe.' So the people dispersed and went into their homes or into the mosque.

A humble victory

On the morning of Friday, 20 Ramadan, 8 A.H., the Messenger of Allah entered Makkah with his head bowed. When he realized the honour of the conquest Allah had bestowed upon him, he felt so humble before Allah that his chin almost touched the back of his camel. He was reciting *Surat al-Fath* as he rode into Makkah in victory. He raised the standard of justice, equality, and humility. Behind him rode Usamah ibn Zayd, the son of his freed slave, rather than any sons of the Banu Hashim or of the Quraysh leaders, even though they were present.

One man, trembling with awe on the Day of the Conquest, was told, 'Be at ease. Do not be afraid. I am not a king. I am only the son of a woman of the Quraysh who used to eat meat dried in the sun.'

Mercy not slaughter

When Sa'd ibn 'Ubadah in the squadron of the Ansar passed by Abu Sufyan he called out, 'Today is a day of slaughter. Today there is no more sanctuary. Today Allah has humbled the Quraysh.'

When the Messenger of Allah's squadron came near Abu Sufyan, he complained, 'Messenger of Allah, did you not hear what Sa'd said?'

'What was that?' said the Messenger of Allah, and Abu Sufyan repeated what Sa'd had called out.

The Messenger of Allah disliked Sa'd's comments and replied, 'Today is a day of mercy and forgiveness when Allah will exalt the Quraysh and raise honour for the Ka'bah.'

He then sent for Sa'd, took the standard from him and gave it to his son Qays. This meant that the standard did not really leave Sa'd because it only went to his son. But Abu Sufyan was satisfied and Sa'd was not too upset.

Small skirmishes

A small skirmish broke out between Safwan ibn Umayyah, 'Ikrimah ibn Abi Jahl and Suhayl ibn 'Amr, who came up against the companions of Khalid ibn al-Walid. Twelve of the idolworshippers were killed when they tried to stop the advance of the Muslim forces. The rest gave in without further bloodshed. The Messenger of Allah had told his men when they entered Makkah, 'Do not fight anyone unless they attack you.'

Purifying the *Haram*

The Messenger of Allah got down from his camel when everything had calmed down. He went to the Ka'bah first and performed *tawaf*. Around the Ka'bah were three hundred and sixty idols. With a stick he was carrying he began to push them over, saying, *'The truth has come and falsehood has vanished away. Falsehood is ever vanishing.'* (17: 81) *'The truth has come and falsehood originates not nor brings again.'* (34: 49) The idols collapsed one by one, falling onto their faces. Pictures and statues were found in the Ka'bah and the Messenger of Allah ordered that they should also be destroyed.

A day of piety

Having performed *tawaf*, the Messenger of Allah called 'Uthman ibn Talhah who had the key of the Ka'bah. The doors were unlocked and he went in. He had asked 'Uthman for the key before the *hijrah* to Madinah but he had received a rude answer and insults. He had shown tolerance by answering, ' 'Uthman, one day you will see this key in my hand. I will then put it where I wish.'

'Uthman had retorted, 'The Quraysh will be destroyed and humiliated on that day.'

'No,' said the Messenger of Allah, 'Rather it will be a day of prosperity and security for the Quraysh.' His words made such an impression on 'Uthman ibn Talhah that he came to believe the prediction would eventually take place.

When the Messenger of Allah came out of the Ka'bah, 'Ali ibn Abi Talib stood up holding the key of the Ka'bah in his hand. He said to the Messenger of Allah, 'Grant us the guardianship of the Ka'bah along with providing water for the pilgrims.'

The Messenger of Allah asked, 'Where is 'Uthman ibn Talhah?'

'Uthman was summoned and the Messenger of Allah said to him, 'Here is your key, 'Uthman. Today is a day of piety and good faith. Keep it forever as an inheritance. Only a tyrant would take it from you.'

Islam: *Tawhid* and unity

The Messenger of Allah opened the door of the Ka'bah. The Quraysh had filled the mosque, and were waiting in rows to see what he would do. Holding the door frame, he said,

> There is no god but Allah alone. He has no partner. He has made good His promise. He has helped His servant and He alone has put all allies to flight. Every claim of privilege, property or bloodline are abolished by me today except for the custody of the Ka'bah and providing water for the pilgrims.
>
> O people of the Quraysh! Allah has abolished the haughtiness of the *Jahiliyyah* and its veneration of ancestors. People all spring from Adam, and Adam came from dust.' Then he recited this verse, *'O mankind, We have created you male and female, and appointed you races and tribes, that you may know one another. Surely the noblest among you in the sight of Allah is the most godfearing of you. Allah is All-Knowing, All-Aware.* (49: 13)

Prophet of Love, Prophet of Mercy

Then the Messenger of Allah said, 'Men of the Quraysh! What do you think I will do to you?'

They said, 'We hope for the best. You are a noble brother and the son of a noble brother!'

He replied, 'I say to you what Yusuf said to his brothers, *"No reproach shall be on you this day."* Go on your way, you are free.'

He ordered Bilal to climb up on the roof of the

Ka'bah and give the *adhan*. It was the first time the leaders of the Quraysh had heard the word of Allah rising up; the valley of Makkah reverberated with the sound. The Messenger of Allah entered the house of Umm Hani bint Abi Talib, had a bath and prayed eight *rak'ats* of *Salatu'l-Fath*, the Prayer of Victory, to thank Allah for the conquest.

No discrimination

In the meantime, Fatimah, a woman of the Banu Makhzum had been apprehended for theft. Her community went to Usamah ibn Zayd, hoping that he could persuade the Messenger of Allah to intercede on her behalf. When he spoke to the Messenger of Allah about it, however, he was put to shame.

'Do you dare to speak to me about one of the *hudud*, the limits laid down by Allah?' the Messenger of Allah asked him.

Usamah beseeched him, 'Pray for my forgiveness, Messenger of Allah!'

That evening the Messenger of Allah made a speech. After praising Allah, he said, 'The people before you were destroyed because when one of their noblemen stole, they ignored the offence but when one of the poor people stole, they administered the *hadd* (prescribed punishment). By the One who holds my life in His hand, if Fatimah bint Muhammad, were to steal, I would have her hand cut off.'

Then he ordered that the woman's right hand be cut off. She genuinely repented of her sin and went on to marry and lead a normal life.

Paying homage in Islam

A large crowd gathered in Makkah to accept Islam and to pay homage to the Messenger of Allah. He received them on Mount Safa where they took the oath of allegiance. They promised to obey Allah and His Messenger to the best of their ability.

When the men had pledged their faith, the women took the oath, including Hind bint 'Utbah, the wife of Abu Sufyan. She was veiled and tried to disguise herself because of what she had done to Hamzah, but the Messenger of Allah recognized her bold talk. 'Forgive what is past and Allah will forgive you,' she said to him.

'My life is with you and my death will be among you'

When Allah opened up Makkah to His Messenger, and he was back in his own homeland and city of birth once more, the Ansar said among themselves, 'Allah has given him power over his homeland and city so he will probably stay here and not return to Madinah.'

The Messenger of Allah asked them what they were talking about. No one else knew about the conversation. At first they were too shy to tell him but eventually they confessed what they had said.

He assured them, 'I seek refuge with Allah! I will live with you and I will die among you.'

Removing all vestiges of idolworship

The Messenger of Allah sent groups of his Companions to destroy the idols standing round the Ka'bah. All of the idols were broken including al-Lat, al-'Uzza, and

Manat. He sent a crier to announce in Makkah, 'Whoever believes in Allah and the Last Day should destroy any idol in his house.' He also sent representatives to the surrounding tribes telling them to destroy their idols.

Then the Messenger of Allah assembled the Muslims in Makkah and declared that the city would be a sanctuary forever. He said, 'It is not lawful for anyone who believes in Allah and the Hereafter to spill blood in the city nor to cut down a tree. It was not lawful for anyone before me nor shall it be lawful for anyone after me.' The Messenger of Allah then returned to Madinah.

Outcome of the conquest of Makkah

The conquest of Makkah had a tremendous impact on the Arabs. It showed that Islam was the religion of Allah and paved the way for the whole of Arabia to accept the faith. From far and wide people came to pay their respects to the Messenger of Allah and to accept Islam at his hands. Allah spoke the truth:

> *When comes the help of Allah and victory and you see people entering the religion of Allah in throngs* (Surah al-Nasr 110: 1–2).

The Battle of Hunayn

The Hawazin

Once Islam was attracting so much popular attention, its enemies made a final attempt to check its expansion. It was the Arabs' last arrow in their quiver against Islam and the Muslims.

The Hawazin regarded themselves as the greatest tribe after the Quraysh. There had always been rivalry between the two. When the Quraysh submitted to the Messenger of Allah in Makkah, the Hawazin became the undisputed champions of the idolworshippers.

Malik ibn 'Awf an-Nasri, the Hawazin chief, called for war against the Muslims and the tribe of Thaqif supported him. They agreed to advance against the Muslims taking their property, women and children with them so that everyone would fight to the last in defence of his family and possessions.

The Messenger of Allah set out with two thousand Muslims from Makkah, including those men who had only recently accepted Islam and some who had not yet accepted the faith, and ten thousand who had set out with him from Madinah. It was the strongest force mobilized so far to defend the honour of Islam. Some Muslims even boasted, 'We will not be defeated today for lack of numbers.'

The valley of Hunayn

The Muslims advanced to the valley of Hunayn before dawn on 10 Shawwal 8 A.H. The Hawazin were already in the valley, concealed in its ravines. The Muslims were terrified when the Hawazin suddenly loosed volleys of arrows, then appeared, unsheathing their swords, to attack as one man.

Many Muslims fled, none paying attention to anyone else. It was a critical moment. A complete rout of the Muslims was in sight. They were unlikely to put up any resistance after what had happened. In addition, a rumour spread among the people that the Prophet had been killed, just as had occurred in the Battle of Uhud, and the Muslim forces retreated still further.

The Hawazin are defeated

Allah had chastized the Muslims for boasting about their strength and had made them taste the bitterness of defeat after the sweetness of victory. They had to remember that both come from Allah. Then the peace of Allah seemed to descend once more. The Messenger of Allah had stayed firm on his white mule; he had not shown any fear. Some of the Muhajirun and Ansar had remained with him. Al-'Abbas ibn 'Abdu'l-Muttalib was holding the bridle of his mule when the Messenger of Allah called out:

'I am the Prophet and there is no denying it. I am the son of 'Abdu'l-Muttalib.'

When a squadron of idolworshippers advanced towards him, he took a handful of dust and threw it at the distant enemy lines. They were blinded by it.

When he saw his own men in confusion, he said, 'O

'Abbas! Shout: Men of Ansar! Comrades of the acacia tree!'

They heard the call and answered, 'At your service! At your service!'

'Abbas had a loud voice which carried well. The soldiers rushed back towards him, dismounting from their camels and taking up their swords and shields. When a large group of them had gathered round the Messenger of Allah, they bore down on the enemy and battle began. The Messenger of Allah stood up in his stirrups and his people took heart. Both sides fought bravely and a group of handcuffed prisoners was brought to the Messenger of Allah and Allah sent down His angels to help. They filled the valley and the Hawazin were defeated. This is referred to in the Qur'an:

> *Allah has already helped you on many fields, and on the day of Hunayn, when your multitude was pleasing to you, but it availed you naught, and the land for all its breadth was straitened for you, and you turned about, retreating. Then Allah sent down His Tranquillity upon His Messenger and upon the believers, and He sent down legions you did not see, and He chastized the unbelievers; that is the recompense of the unbelievers.* (9: 25–6)

The Expedition of Ta'if

The siege of the Thaqif

The soldiers of Thaqif who had escaped from Hunayn retreated to Ta'if. They locked the city gates after storing sufficient provisions for a year. Then they prepared for war against the Muslims. The Messenger of Allah and his army went to Ta'if at once and pitched camp outside the city wall. The gates remained locked against them. The Thaqif, who were good archers, shot so many arrows at the Muslims that the air seemed to be filled as if with a swarm of locusts.

The Muslims moved their camp back out of range of the arrows and laid siege to Ta'if. For more than twenty days heavy fighting continued and volleys of arrows were exchanged. In this prolonged siege the Messenger of Allah used a catapult for the first time. The enemy arrows took their toll of several Muslims' lives.

When the siege was tight and the battle showed no signs of ending, the Messenger of Allah commanded that the vineyards of the Thaqif be cut down. The enemy relied on these fine grapes for their livelihood. When the Thaqif begged him to spare the vines, the Messenger of Allah replied, 'I will leave them to Allah and kinship between us.'

He ordered that an announcement be made, 'Any

slave who comes out to us is free.' About ten men came out.

The Messenger of Allah had not been given leave by Allah to conquer Ta'if so he told 'Umar ibn al-Khattab to declare that the siege was over and the army could depart. The announcement caused an uproar and soldiers said, 'We are leaving without conquering Ta'if!'

The Messenger of Allah said, 'Alright, go and fight.'

They attacked the enemy but many Muslims were wounded.

The Messenger of Allah then said, 'We are going tomorrow, Allah willing,' and this time they felt relief.

The booty of Hunayn

On his way back from Ta'if, the Messenger of Allah stopped at al-Ji'irranah with his army. He waited for more than ten days for the Hawazin to come to him to say they had accepted Islam. When this did not happen, he began to distribute the spoils. The first people he gave to were the *Mu'allafat-al-Qulub*, those whose hearts still needed to be won.

Returning the captives

A delegation of fourteen Hawazin came to the Messenger of Allah and requested him to return to them their kinsmen and property. He replied, 'You see the people with me? What I love most is the truth. Which are dearest to you, your children and your wives or your property?'

In unison they said, 'We do not consider anything equal to our children and wives.'

He advised them, 'Rise tomorrow when I pray and

say, "We seek the intercession of the Messenger of Allah with the Muslims and we seek the intercession of the Muslims with the Messenger of Allah to return our wives and children to us." '

When he prayed *Zuhr,* they got up and did as they had been advised. The Messenger of Allah then said, 'As for what belongs to me and the Banu 'Abdu'l-Muttalib, it is yours, and I will make a recommendation to others for you.'

The Muhajirun and Ansar said, 'What we have belongs to the Messenger of Allah.'

Three of the Banu Tamim, Banu Fazarah and Banu Sulaym refused to hand over their shares. The Messenger of Allah said to them, 'These people have come as Muslims. I waited for them and I gave them a choice but they do not consider anything equal to their children and wives. Whoever has any of them and is happy to return them he should do just that. Whoever wants to keep his captives should also return them and he will be given six shares in exchange from the first booty Allah gives us.'

Everyone replied, 'We are content with the Messenger of Allah.'

He said, 'I do not know who among you is pleased and who is not. You go back now and your chief will tell correctly about your affairs.' All of them returned their captives' women and children to them so that none of them were left behind. The Messenger of Allah made a gift of a garment to each released captive.

A noble gesture

Among those who were brought to the Messenger of Allah was ash-Shayma' bint Halimah as-Sa'diyah, his foster-sister. She had been treated roughly as they did not know who she was. When she said that she was the milk-sister of their companion, they did not believe her.

When ash-Shayma' was taken to the Messenger of Allah, she said, 'Messenger of Allah! I am your foster-sister!'

He said, 'Can you prove that?'

She replied, 'I still have the scar where you bit me on my back when I was carrying you.'

The Messenger of Allah recognized the mark. He spread out his cloak for her to sit on, and treated her courteously.

He said, 'If you like, you may live with me in affection and honour or, if you wish, I will give you provision and you can go back to your people.'

She said, 'Give me provision and return me to my people.'

She accepted Islam before she left, taking with her three slaves, a slavegirl, and some cattle and sheep.

The Thaqif's decision

When the Muslims were returning from Ta'if, the Messenger of Allah asked the Muslims to recite, 'We are returning, repenting, worshipping and glorifying our Lord.'

Some said, 'Messenger of Allah, curse the Thaqif!'

He raised his hands and entreated, 'O Allah, guide the Thaqif to the right path and bring them here.'

'Urwah ibn Mas'ud ath-Thaqafi caught up with the Messenger of Allah before he entered Madinah. He became a Muslim and returned to invite his people to Islam. He was very popular and well-respected in his tribe, but when he called them to Islam, they turned against him. They shot arrows at him; one hit him and he was killed as a martyr.

The Thaqif held out for some months after killing 'Urwah, but after taking counsel among themselves, they decided that they had no hope of defeating all the Arab tribes around them which had accepted Islam. They decided to send a delegation to the Messenger of Allah.

No leniency

When the Thaqif arrived, a tent was pitched for them in a corner of the mosque. They accepted Islam and asked the Messenger of Allah to let them keep their idol al-Lat for three years. The Messenger of Allah refused. But they continued to ask him, first for two years and then for one. Still he refused. Finally they asked for it for one month after their return. He refused this too, and sent Abu Sufyan ibn Harb and al-Mughirah ibn Shu'bah, one of their people, to destroy it. The Thaqif also asked the Messenger of Allah to excuse them from offering prayers. He told them, 'Nothing remains in a religion without prayer.'

After the delegation returned home, Islam spread among the Thaqif until every last person in Ta'if was a Muslim.

The Tabuk Expedition

The Arabs had never thought of fighting or attacking the Romans. They probably considered themselves to be not strong enough for that task.

The Romans, however, remembered the Mu'tah expedition and were still a threat. The Messenger of Allah decided to lead a Muslim army into Roman territory before the Roman armies crossed the Arab borders and threatened the heart of Islam.

The Tabuk expedition took place in Rajab, 9 A.H. The Messenger of Allah led the expedition in intense heat, when the dates were ripe and the shade of the trees was pleasant. It was a long journey through arid deserts towards a vast enemy army. He had made the position clear to the Muslims in advance so that they could make preparations for the journey. It was a difficult time because the Muslims were experiencing a severe drought.

The hypocrites made various excuses not to accompany the Messenger of Allah. They said they feared the enemy or the intense heat. They were reluctant to perform *jihad* and had doubts about the truth. Allah Almighty said of them: *'Those who were left behind rejoiced in tarrying behind the Messenger of Allah and were averse to struggling with their possessions and their selves in the way of Allah. They said, "Go not forth in the heat." Say: "The Fire of Jahannam is hotter, did they but understand!"'* (9: 81)

The Companions' response to *jihad*

In preparing for the expedition, the Messenger of Allah had encouraged the wealthy to spend in the way of Allah. Some provided mounts for those who had neither provision nor mount, expecting a reward from Allah. 'Uthman ibn 'Affan spent one thousand dinars on the 'Army of Distress' and the Messenger of Allah prayed for him.

The army travels to Tabuk

The Messenger of Allah set out for Tabuk with 30,000 men from Madinah. It was the largest Muslim army ever to set forth on an expedition.

When they reached al-Hijr, the land of Thamud, he told the Companions that it was a country of those who were being punished for their sins.

'If you enter the houses of those who did wrong, enter tearfully, fearing that what befell them might also befall you.' He added that they must not drink any of al-Hijr's water nor use it for ablutions. Because the soldiers had no water they complained to the Messenger of Allah. He prayed to Allah and a dark cloud brought rain so that everyone could quench their thirst and store sufficient water for their needs.

The Messenger of Allah returns to Madinah

When the Messenger of Allah reached Tabuk, the Arab amirs on the borders called on him and made treaties of peace. They also paid to him the *jizyah* tax. The Messenger of Allah guaranteed their borders, the security of their territories and their caravans and ships travelling by land and sea. Letters to this effect were delivered to all parties.

Then came the news that the Romans had withdrawn from the border towns. They had decided not to encroach on Muslim land. The Prophet could see no reason to pursue them into their own territory as his goal had already been achieved.

He stayed at Tabuk for about two weeks and then travelled back to Madinah.

The trial of Ka'b ibn Malik

Among those who had stayed behind at the time of this expedition were Ka'b ibn Malik, Murarah ibn ar-Rabi' and Hilal ibn Umayyah. They were among the first Muslims and had been thoroughly tested in Islam. Murarah ibn ar-Rabi' and Hilal ibn Umayyah had been present at Badr and it was not their nature to not take part in the battle. The situation was only part of the Divine wisdom, so they would really examine themselves and be a lesson for all Muslims in the future. Such failings are usually because of procrastination, weak will and over-reliance on means.

The Messenger of Allah forbade anyone to speak to them. All the Muslims obeyed him and people avoided them. They had to endure that trial for fifty days. Ka'b ibn Malik would attend prayers with the Muslims and visit the markets but everyone ignored him. But his suffering only increased his faith in Islam.

The wives of these three were also affected by the measures and no one was allowed to go near them either.

A further test came when the influential King of Ghassan heard what was happening in Madinah. He invited Ka'b ibn Malik to his court in order to honour him and lure him from Islam. But when the King's messenger delivered the invitation to Ka'b he threw it into the fire.

Allah's examination was over and none of the three had failed the test. A revelation came from Allah to illustrate how their example would hold for all time. They had not deserted their faith but had found refuge and safety with Allah. The Qur'an says:

> *Allah has turned towards the Prophet and the Muhajirun and the Ansar who followed him in the hour of difficulty, after the hearts of a party of them almost swerved aside; then He turned towards them; surely He is Gentle to them, and he turned to the three who remained behind, until, when the earth became straitened for them, for all its breadth, and their souls became straitened for them, and they thought that there was no shelter from Allah except in Him, then He turned towards them, that they might also turn; surely Allah turns, and is Compassionate.* (9: 117–18)

Tabuk: the last expedition

The expedition to Tabuk, in Rajab 9 A.H., was the last in the Messenger of Allah's campaign. In all, the Muslims had fought in twenty-seven battles and taken part in sixty forays and expeditions. No conqueror had ever achieved such success with so little loss of life. Throughout the campaign a total of only one thousand and eighteen from both sides had been killed. Only Allah knows the number of those whose lives were spared in gaining security for the Arabian peninsula. Eventually it was so safe that a woman pilgrim could travel all the way from Hirah to Makkah without fearing anyone except Allah.

The first *hajj*

The *hajj* was made obligatory in 9 A.H. The Messenger of Allah sent Abu Bakr as amir for the *hajj* in that year. Three hundred men from Madinah went to Makkah with him. The Messenger of Allah sent for 'Ali ibn Abi Talib and said to him, 'Go out and announce to the people on the Day of Sacrifice that "no *kafir* will enter Paradise and after this year no idolworshipper will perform *hajj* nor do *tawaf* if he is in a state of nudity.'

The Year of Delegations

Delegations

After Makkah had been conquered and the Prophet had returned victorious from Tabuk, Arab delegations began to pour into the heartland of Islam. They learned about Islam, saw the character of the Messenger of Allah, and the life-style of his Companions. Tents were erected for them in the courtyard of the mosque; they heard the Qur'an recited; watched the Muslims praying and asked the Messenger of Allah to explain the faith· to them. He impressed them with his eloquence and wisdom, and he constantly quoted verses from the Qur'an. They believed what they heard and were well satisfied. They returned to their homes full of zeal, calling on their people to accept Islam and decrying paganism and its negative effects.

Dimam ibn Tha'labah came to Madinah representing the Banu Sa'd ibn Bakr. He was a Muslim when he returned to his people and he was determined to invite them to Islam.

The first thing he said to them was, 'Al-Lat and al-'Uzza are evil!'

They answered in alarm, 'Stop, Dimam! Beware of leprosy. Beware of elephantiasis! Beware of madness!'

He said, 'Confound you! By Allah, they can neither hurt nor heal. Allah has sent a Messenger and given a Book to him through which He seeks to deliver you from your sorry state. I testify that there is no god but Allah without any associate and that Muhammad is His slave and Messenger. I have brought you what He has commanded you to do and what He has forbidden you.'

Before that night was over there was not a man or a woman in his tribe who had not become a Muslim.

'Adi the son of Hatim, whose generosity was well-known, came to Madinah. He became a Muslim after witnessing the character and humility of the Messenger of Allah.

'By Allah!' he said, 'This has nothing to do with the way all the kings behave.'

The Messenger of Allah sent Mu'adh ibn Jabal and Abu Musa to Yemen to invite the people to Islam and he advised them, 'Make things easy and not difficult. Cheer them up and do not make them afraid.'

The obligation of *Zakat*

In the ninth year of the *hijrah*, Allah made *zakat* obligatory upon the Muslims.

The Farewell *Hajj*

The Prophet's Farewell *Hajj*

When Allah had purified the Ka'bah from desecration and the idols were destroyed, the Muslims yearned to perform *hajj* again. The mission of the Messenger of Allah was also nearing completion and it was necessary for him to bid farewell to his loving Companions. So Allah gave permission to His Messenger to take them for *hajj*. It was the first *hajj* for him since he began his mission.

He left Madinah for many reasons: to perform *hajj*; to meet Muslims from far and near; to teach them their faith and its rituals; to bear witness to the truth; to hand over the trust; and to give his final instructions. He would administer an oath binding on the Muslims to follow his teachings and to be rid of the last traces of *Jahiliyyah*. More than a hundred thousand Muslims performed *hajj* with him. This is known as *Hajjat al-Wada'* (the 'Farewell *Hajj*') and *Hajjat al-Balagh* (the '*Hajj* of Conveying').

The Prophet performs *Hajj*

Once the Messenger of Allah had decided to go on *hajj* he informed the people of his intention and they started to prepare for the journey.

When news of it spread outside Madinah, people

flocked to the city wanting to go on *hajj* with the Messenger of Allah. Huge throngs also joined him on the way. The crowds stretched in front of him, behind him, and to his right and left as far as the eye could see. He left Madinah on Saturday, 25 Dhu'l-Qa'dah, after praying four *rak'ats* for *Zuhr*. Before the prayer, in a sermon, he explained the essentials of putting on *ihram,* the pilgrim dress, and the obligations and *sunan* of the *hajj.*

As he departed he said the *talbiyah*: 'At Your service, O Allah, at Your service! You have no partner. At Your service! Praise and Blessing are Yours and the Kingdom. You have no associate.' The crowd chanted the *talbiyah* along with him as they continued their journey.

He entered Makkah on 4 Dhu'l-Hijjah and went straight to the *Masjid al-Haram.* He performed *tawaf* of the Ka'bah and the *sa'y* between Safa and Marwah. He stayed in Makkah for four days and then on the Day of *Tarwiyah,* 8 Dhu'l-Hijjah, he made for Mina with his Companions. He prayed *Zuhr* and *'Asr* there and spent the night.

At sunrise on 9 Dhu'l-Hijjah, he left Mina and made for 'Arafat followed by all the pilgrims. It was a Friday. Down in the valley, he delivered a great *khutbah* to the people while seated on his camel. He confirmed the principles of Islam and struck at the roots of idolworship and *Jahiliyyah.* He commanded the people to treat as inviolable and sacrosanct those issues on which all religions agree – life, property, and honour.

He declared that all the customs of *Jahiliyyah* were trampled under foot and that all usury was eliminated and made void. He commanded that people treat women well and he mentioned the rights men have over women and those which women have over men, adding that it was obligatory to provide food and clothing for them.

He commanded his community to hold fast to the Book of Allah; as long as they did this they would not be misguided, he said. Finally, he told them that on the Day of Judgement Allah would ask them about him. He asked them to bear witness that he had conveyed to them the message as he had been commanded.

They replied as one voice, 'We testify that you have conveyed the message and that you have fulfilled your task.'

He pointed to the sky and called on Allah three times to bear witness to it. Then he commanded those present to convey the message to those who were absent.

When the *khutbah* was over, he called on Bilal to give the *adhan*. Then the *iqamah* was given and he prayed *Zuhr* with two *rak'ats* and after the *iqamah* for *'Asr* had been given he prayed that, too, with two *rak'ats*.

When he had finished the prayers, he mounted his camel and rode until he came to *Mawqif*, the halting place at 'Arafat. Remaining on his camel, he made supplication, prayed and glorified Allah until sunset. In his supplication he raised his hands to his chest, like a pauper begging for food, and pleaded,

> O Allah, You hear my words and You see where I am. You know my secrets and what I reveal. Nothing can be hidden from You. I am the poor unfortunate who seeks help and protection. I am fearful and apprehensive, confessing and acknowledging my wrong actions.
>
> I ask You as a poor wretch asks and I entreat You with the entreaty of a humble, sinful person. I make supplication to You as a fearful, blind person does; one who bows low before You and whose

eyes overflow with tears for You, whose body is humble and who is powerless against You. O Allah, do not make me despair in my calling on You, Lord. Be merciful and compassionate to me, O best of those who are asked and best of givers!

Then it was revealed to him: *'Today I have perfected your religion for you, and I have completed My blessing on you, and I have approved Islam for your religion.'* (5: 3)

At sunset, the Messenger of Allah moved from 'Arafat to Muzdalifah. There he prayed *Maghrib* and *'Isha'* and then slept until morning. At dawn he prayed *Fajr* for its first time then rode until he came to the *Mash'ar al-Haram* the sacred site at Muzdalifah. He faced the *qiblah* and began to make supplications. He recited the *takbir* ('Allah is great') and the *tahlil* ('There is no god but Allah'). He left Muzdalifah before sunrise and travelled quickly to the *Jamrat al-'Aqabah* at Mina, and threw pebbles at this symbol of Shaytan.

He delivered a meaningful sermon in Mina in which he informed the Muslims of the sanctity of the Day of Sacrifice, of its inviolability and its favour with Allah. He also reminded them of the sanctity of Makkah over all other cities. He commanded them to obey their leaders according to the Book of Allah; to adopt the *hajj* practices he had used; and not to revert to being unbelievers after his time or to start fighting amongst themselves. He commanded that they pass on his words. 'Worship your Lord, pray your five prayers, fast your month, and obey the One in command and you will enter the Garden of your Lord,' he said. Then he bade the people farewell. Thus this *hajj* was named 'The *Hajj* of Farewell.'

Next, the Messenger of Allah went to the place of

sacrifice at Mina and sacrificed sixty-three camels, one for each year of his life. He commanded 'Ali to sacrifice the rest of the hundred camels brought from Madinah. When the Prophet had finished making the sacrifice, he called for the barber and had his head shaved. He divided his hair between those who were near him. Then he rode to Makkah and performed *tawaf al-Ifadah,* which is also called *tawaf az-Ziarah.* At the well of Zamzam he drank while standing before returning to Mina that same day where he spent the night. The next morning he waited until the sun had declined before going to perform the ritual stoning of Shaytan. He started with the stoning of *Jamrat-al-'Ula,* then of *Jamrat-al-Wusta* and lastly of *Jamrat-al-'Aqabah.* This was repeated over the three days of *ayyam at-Tashriq* following the Day of Sacrifice.

After the three days of *Tashriq,* he went to Makkah and performed the *tawaf* of Farewell before dawn. Then he asked his Companions to prepare for their departure to Madinah. On their return journey they stayed the night at Dhu'l-Hulayfah.

When he first saw Madinah on his return from Makkah, he recited the *takbir* three times and then said,

> There is no god but Allah, alone with no partner. His is the kingdom and His is the praise. He has power over all things. We are returning, repenting, worshipping, prostrating to our Lord, and praising Him. Allah has been true to His promise and has helped His slave and defeated the enemies alone.'

He entered Madinah in broad daylight.

The Death of the Messenger of Allah

Completion of his task

When Islam reached the pinnacle of perfection, these words were sent down by Allah: *'Today I have perfected your religion for you, and I have completed My blessing on you, and I have approved Islam for your religion.'* (5: 3) The Messenger of Allah had conveyed the message truthfully, he had fulfilled the trust placed in him and had striven for Allah as he should. Allah had delighted His Prophet when people entered Islam in throngs. At this stage, Allah gave His Prophet permission to leave this world and the hour of meeting drew near. Allah announced:

> *When comes the help of Allah and victory and you see people entering into the religion of Allah in throngs, then glorify the praise of your Lord and ask His forgiveness. He is Ever-turning.* (110: 1–3)

The Prophet's illness

The Messenger of Allah was taken ill shortly before the end of Safar. During the night he had been to Baqi' al-Gharqad, a cemetery in Madinah now called al-Baqi', to pray for the dead. The following morning he became ill.

'A'ishah, *Umm al-Mu'minin* (may Allah be pleased with her) said, 'The Messenger of Allah returned from al-Baqi' and found me suffering from a headache. I was saying, "O my head!" He said, "Rather, by Allah, 'A'ishah, *my* head!"'

His pain increased. Then, in the house of Maymunah, he called his wives and asked them to permit him to be nursed in 'A'ishah's house. All of them agreed. He came out walking between two men of his family, Fadl ibn 'Abbas and 'Ali ibn Abi Talib. His head was bandaged and his feet were dragging as he entered 'A'ishah's house.

'A'ishah said that during his final illness, he told her, ' 'A'ishah, I still feel pain from the food I ate at Khaybar. I feel my aorta being cut because of that poison.'

The last expedition

The Messenger of Allah had ordered Usamah ibn Zayd ibn Harithah to lead an expedition to Syria, commanding him to take the cavalry to the borders of al-Balqa' and ad-Darun in Palestine.

Many of the leading Muhajirun and Ansar were in his army, the most eminent being 'Umar ibn al-Khattab. The Prophet's illness took a serious turn when the army was at the border of al-Jurf. After his death, Abu Bakr sent forward the army under Usamah in order to carry out the Prophet's last wishes and to fulfil what he had wanted.

During his illness, the Messenger of Allah told the Muslims to offer hospitality to the delegations in the way that he had and to be generous with their gifts to them. They should not allow two religions to co-exist but should expel the idolworshippers from the Arabian peninsula.

A caution

One day while he was ill, a group of Muslims gathered in 'A'ishah's house. The Messenger of Allah welcomed them and prayed for their guidance on the right path, their victory and their success. He said, 'I advise you to fear Allah and I pray for Allah to watch over you. I am a clear warner to you from Him. Do not be arrogant where Allah's servants and habitations are concerned. Allah has said to me and to you, *"That is the Last Abode; We appoint it for those who desire not exorbitance in the earth, nor corruption. The ultimate issue is to the godfearing."* (28: 83) and *"Is there not in Jahannam a lodging for those who are proud?"* (39: 60)'

An ascetic

'A'ishah said that the Messenger of Allah said during his final illness, ' 'A'ishah, what have you done with the gold?' When she brought a few coins to him, he began to turn them over in his hand and said, 'What could Muhammad say to his Lord if he were to meet Him with these? Give them away!'

Concern for the prayer

The pain was hard for the Messenger of Allah to bear. He asked, 'Have the people prayed?' Those with him answered, 'No, they are waiting for you, Messenger of Allah.'

He said, 'Pour some water into a basin for me.'

When they took it to him, he washed and tried to get up, but he fainted. When he regained consciousness, he asked, 'Have the people prayed?'

'No, they are waiting for you, Messenger of Allah.'

'Pour some water into a basin for me.'

He washed again and tried to get up, but once again he fainted. When he regained consciousness, he asked, 'Have the people prayed?'

Once more he was told, 'No, they are waiting for you, Messenger of Allah.'

He again said, 'Pour some water into a basin for me.'

He washed and struggled to get up, but once more he fainted. When he came to he asked, 'Have the people prayed?'

'No, they are waiting for you, Messenger of Allah.'

Concern for the *imamah* of Abu Bakr

The people were sitting quietly in the mosque waiting for the Messenger of Allah to lead the *'Isha'* prayer. However, he sent for Abu Bakr to lead it instead. Abu Bakr, a tender-hearted man, said, ''Umar, you lead the prayer!'

'Umar replied, 'You are more qualified to do it.' So Abu Bakr led the people in prayer during that period.

When the Messenger of Allah felt better he went out for the *Zuhr* prayer supported by two men, al-'Abbas and 'Ali ibn Abi Talib (may Allah be pleased with them). When Abu Bakr saw him arrive, he began to move back but the Messenger of Allah motioned to him not to move. He asked al-'Abbas and 'Ali to seat him by Abu Bakr who prayed standing while the Messenger of Allah prayed sitting.

The Farewell Address

Sitting on the *minbar* with his head bandaged the Messenger of Allah said, 'Allah gave one of His slaves the choice between this world or that which is with Him. His slave chose that which is with Allah.' Abu Bakr realized that the Messenger of Allah was referring to himself and broke into tears, saying, 'We will ransom you with ourselves and our sons.'

A last look

Abu Bakr led the Muslims in prayer until the Monday morning. While the Muslims performed the *Fajr* prayer, the Prophet lifted up the curtain of 'A'ishah's door and gazed at them standing before their Lord. He saw the fruits of his efforts to call people to Islam and *jihad* and Allah knew how happy he was. His face was beaming with joy.

The Companions said, 'He lifted the curtain of 'A'ishah's room and stared at us while he was standing there. It was as if his face was an open page of the Qur'an; he smiled and we were put to the test by getting carried away with our delight. We thought he might be coming out to the prayer but he indicated to us to finish it. He then pulled the curtain down. That was the day on which he died.'

A warning

One of the last pronouncements of the Messenger of Allah was, 'May Allah fight the Jews and Christians! They turned the graves of their Prophets into places of worship. Two religions should not remain in the land of the Arabs.'

'A'ishah and Ibn 'Abbas said, 'When the Messenger of Allah was ill, he drew up his cloak over his face. When he was distressed, he uncovered his face and while he was like that, he said, "May Allah curse the Jews and the Christians who turned the graves of their Prophets into places of worship." He was warning the Muslims against that practice.'

The final instructions

When the Messenger of Allah was close to death, he repeated, 'Be careful of prayer and those in your charge.' Then his breast began to heave and his speech became inaudible.

'Ali said, 'The Messenger of Allah commended the prayer and *zakat* to Muslims and to be generous to those in their charge.'

'A'ishah said: 'When he had his fatal illness I started reciting *al-Mu'awwidhatayn* as he used to do when he was ill. He raised his eyes to the Heaven and said: "With the Highest Companion, with the Highest Companion".'

She added: 'Just at that moment, 'Abdu'r-Rahman ibn Abi Bakr came in with a small, green, freshly-cut twig in his hand. The Messenger of Allah looked at it and I thought that he wanted to use it as a *miswak*. I took it and chewed it to make it soft and pliable, then I handed it to him. He rubbed his teeth with it thoroughly. Then just as he tried to hand it back to me it fell from his hand.'

She also said, 'In front of him was a small pot of water. He dipped his hand into it and wiped his face, saying, "There is no god but Allah. Verily there are pangs of death." Then he raised his forefinger and began to say, "The Highest Companion, the Highest Companion!" until he died and his hand slipped into the water.'

'A'ishah described his last moments: 'The Messenger of Allah was ill and his head rested on my thigh. He fainted and then regained consciousness and looked up at the ceiling. He said, "O Allah, the Highest Companion." Those were the last words that the Messenger of Allah spoke.'

Leaving this world

When the Messenger of Allah left this world, he controlled the entire Arabian peninsula and kings feared him. Yet he left not a dinar or dirham, not a male or female slave, nothing except his white mule, some weapons and a piece of land he had already given away as *sadaqah*, charity.

His armour had been pawned with a Jew for thirty *sa's* of barley. He had been unable to find anything with which to redeem it before he died.

During his illness, the Messenger of Allah set free forty slaves. He asked 'A'ishah to give away as *sadaqah* the six or seven dinars she was keeping for him.

'A'ishah has related, 'When the Messenger of Allah died, there was nothing in the house that a living creature could eat except a little barley on a shelf. It lasted for a long time until I weighed it and then it finished.'

The Messenger of Allah died on Monday, 12 Rabi' al-Awwal, 11 A.H. in the heat of the afternoon. He was sixty-three years old. It was the darkest, hardest and most difficult day for the Muslims and an affliction for mankind just as his birth had been the happiest day on which the sun ever rose.

Anas and Abu Sa'id al-Khudri said, 'The day on which the Messenger of Allah came to Madinah was the most radiant ever known but the day on which he died was the darkest ever.'

When people saw Umm Ayman weeping they asked why. She answered, 'I knew that the Messenger of Allah would die, but I weep for the revelation from heaven which has been taken from us.'

News of his death

News of the death of the Messenger of Allah descended on the Companions like a thunderbolt. They were stunned because of their intense love for him. They had become used to his loving care for them just as children are assured of the protection of their parents, but even more so. Of his concern Allah Almighty says, *'Now there has come to you a Messenger from among yourselves: grievous to him is your suffering: anxious is he over you, gentle to the believers, compassionate.'* (9: 128)

Every one of his Companions reckoned that he was more gracious and considerate to him than to any other Companion. Some of them could hardly believe the news of his death. 'Umar ibn al-Khattab (may Allah be pleased with him) rebuked the person who told him and then he went to the mosque and addressed the people, saying, 'The Messenger of Allah, may Allah bless him and grant him peace, will not die until Allah annihilates the hypocrites.'

Abu Bakr

Abu Bakr, a man of determination and courage, was needed at this difficult hour. He rushed out from his house when the news reached him. At the door of the mosque he stopped briefly and heard 'Umar addressing the people. Then he went straight to 'A'ishah's room where the Messenger of Allah lay covered with a cloak. He uncovered his face and kissed him, saying, 'You are dearer to me than my father and mother. You have tasted the death which Allah has decreed for you. A second death will never overtake you.' He replaced the cloak over the Messenger of Allah's face and returned to the mosque. He found 'Umar still speaking to the people. He called softly, ' 'Umar, be quiet.'

'Umar was too excited to listen and went on talking. Abu Bakr realized that 'Umar was not in a mood to pay attention, so he stepped forward to speak. When the people heard his voice, they came over to him, leaving 'Umar. Abu Bakr praised Allah and then said, 'O people! If anyone worships Muhammad, tell him that Muhammad is dead. But if anyone worships Allah, then Allah is alive and does not die.'

Then he recited this verse: *'Muhammad is only a Messenger. Messengers have passed away before him. Why, if he should die or is slain, will you turn about on your heels? If any man should turn about on his heels, he will not harm God in any way; and God will recompense the thankful.'* (3: 144)

One man who witnessed the scene in the mosque, commented, 'By Allah, it was as if the people did not know that this verse had been sent down until Abu Bakr recited it on that day. They listened to it and from then on it was always on their lips.'

'Umar said, 'By Allah, when I heard Abu Bakr recite the verse, I was dumbfounded. I fell down as if my legs would not hold me up. I knew that the Messenger of Allah, may Allah bless him and grant him peace, was dead.'

Abu Bakr is paid homage as caliph

In the Hall of Banu Sa'idah, the Muslims paid homage to Abu Bakr as the successor to the Messenger of Allah. They were anxious to prevent devilish intrigues from destroying their unity. They were determined that the Messenger of Allah would leave this world with the Muslims unified and under a strong leader who could take charge of their affairs.

Farewell to the Messenger of Allah

The initial shock and grief experienced by the community were replaced by tranquillity and confidence. They concentrated on the task for which the Messenger of Allah had trained them, beginning with the preparations for his burial.

After members of his family had finished washing and shrouding his body, they placed it in a bier in his house. Abu Bakr told them that he had heard the Messenger of Allah say, 'No Prophet dies but that he is buried where he dies.'

The Messenger of Allah's bed, in which he had died, was removed and a grave dug beneath it by Abu Talhah al-Ansari.

The people came to pay their respects and to say the funeral prayer over him. They came in groups. First the men entered, then the women and lastly the children. No one acted as *Imam* for his funeral prayer.

A sad day

The Messenger of Allah's death heralded a sad day in Madinah. When Bilal gave the *adhan* for *Fajr,* he could not mention the Prophet without breaking down. Hearing his sobs increased the Muslims' sorrow. They were used to listening to the *adhan* while the Messenger of Allah was in this world. Umm Salamah, the *Umm al-Mu'minin,* said, 'What an affliction it was! No distress which befell us after that could compare with our loss of him, may Allah bless him and grant him peace.'

The Prophet had once said, 'O people! Whoever of the people – or believers – has any affliction, they should take comfort by remembering their loss of me. None of my community will ever suffer a greater loss than my death.'

The Prophet's wives

Khadijah bint Khuwaylid al-Qurashiyyah al-Asadiyyah (may Allah be pleased with her) was the first of the Prophet's wives. He married her before his prophethood when she was forty. She died three years before the *hijrah.* She bore him all of his children except for Ibrahim.

After her death he married Sawdah bint Zam'ah al-Qurashiyyah. Later he was wedded to 'A'ishah as-Siddiqah bint Abi Bakr as-Siddiq who was the most intelligent and knowledgeable of the women of the *Ummah.* Hafsah bint 'Umar ibn al-Khattab was his next wife, followed by Zaynab bint Khuzaymah who died two months later. He then married Umm Salamah, Hind bint Abi Umayyah al-Qurashiyyah al-Makhzumiyyah who was the last of his wives to die. He also married Zaynab bint Jahsh, the daughter of his aunt Umaymah. He married Juwayriyyah bint al-Harith ibn Abi Dirar al-Mustaliqiyyah, Umm Habibah bint Abi Sufyan and Safiyyah bint Huyayy ibn Akhtab, chief of the Banu'n-Nadir. His last wife was Maymunah bint al-Harith al-Hilaliyyah. When he died he had nine wives; only Khadijah and Zaynab bint Khuzaymah had died during his lifetime. All of them, except 'A'ishah, had been widows when he married them. Two bondswomen also survived. They were Mariyah bint Sham'un, the Egyptian Copt who had been presented to him by Muqawqis, the ruler of Egypt, and who was the mother of his son Ibrahim, and Rayhanah bint Zayd, of the Banu'n-Nadir. When she became a Muslim, the Messenger of Allah set her free and married her.

The Prophet's children

Khadijah bore him al-Qasim, by whom the Prophet had his *kunyah*; he was called Abul Qasim the father of al-Qasim. He died in infancy. Then Khadijah bore the Prophet four daughters: Zaynab, Ruqayyah, Umm Kulthum, Fatimah, and another son, 'Abdullah, who was known as at-Tayyib and at-Tahir. Fatimah was the Prophet's most beloved daughter. Of Fatimah, he said that she would be the leader of the women in Paradise. She married 'Ali ibn Abi Talib, the son of the Messenger of Allah's uncle. She had two sons, Hasan and Husayn, about whom the Messenger of Allah said, 'Al-Hasan and al-Husayn are the leaders of the youths in Paradise.'

Mariyah the Copt was the mother of Ibrahim who died while still an infant. When he died, the Prophet said in sorrow, 'The eye weeps and the heart is sad, but we do not say anything to incur the anger of Allah. We are sad, O Ibrahim.'

The Prophet's Character and Qualities

'Ali ibn Abi Talib was among those nearest to the Messenger of Allah who knew him best. He described him thus: 'He was not coarse or obscene and he did not shout in the market-place. He did not return evil for evil, but was glad to forgive and forget. He did not lay his hands on anyone save in *jihad* and he did not strike anybody, neither a servant nor a woman. I never saw him take revenge for any offence so long as it was not violating the honour of Allah. When a limitation set by Allah was violated, however, he would be more enraged than anyone else. Given a choice between two courses he would always choose the easier of the two.

'When he entered his house, he behaved like other men. He cleaned his own garments, milked his goat, and carried out household chores.

'He never stood up or sat down without the name of Allah being on his lips. Wherever he went, he would sit at the back of the gathering and he instructed others to do the same. He gave all those who sat with him such attention that they believed that he paid more heed to them than to anyone else. When someone sat with him, he stayed attentive and patient until it was time for that person to depart. When someone asked him for help, he would either give him what he needed or speak kindly to him.

'He was always cheerful and tender-hearted. Everyone regarded him as their father, and he treated everyone as equals.

'He was the most generous of people, the most truthful, the kindest, and the noblest. Those seeing him for the first time were overawed, but those who knew him well loved him. Someone describing him said, "I did not see his like before him or after him." '

Allah endowed His Prophet with elegance and grace and bestowed on him love and dignity. Al-Bara' ibn 'Azib described him, saying, 'The Messenger of Allah was of medium height. I once saw him wearing a red striped robe and I have never seen anything more beautiful than he.'

Abu Hurayrah described him, saying, 'He was on the tall side of medium, with very white skin. His hair was black, and he had excellent front teeth. His eyelashes were long and his shoulders broad.' He went on to say, 'I have never seen a man like him before or since.'

Anas said, 'I have never touched silk finer or softer than the palm of the Messenger of Allah's hand; and I have never smelled any scent more fragrant than his natural odour.'

WORKBOOK

The Age of Ignorance

1. Name five of the religions that preceded the advent of Islam. Briefly explain how each one had gone astray.
2. Describe in detail the lifestyle of the Arabs before the advent of Islam.
3. Explain why the Arabs were best suited to receive the call of Islam.
4. What was the significance of the Ka'bah in Makkah?
5. Explain how *tawhid* contrasts sharply with idol worship.

Before Prophethood

1. Why has the water of Zamzam always been regarded as precious?
2. In your own words, write the story of what took place when the Prophet Ibrahim tried to sacrifice his son, Isma'il.
3. Why was it necessary for the Prophet Isma'il to survive?

4. The Prophet Ibrahim and his son, Isma'il, made three pleas to Allah. What were they?
5. From whose family did the Prophet Muhammad descend?
6. How did 'Amr ibn Luhayy, chief of the Quraysh, lead the people away from Allah?
7. In your own words, write down what took place in the confrontation between the Arabs and the King of Abyssinia's governor, Abrahah, in the Year of the Elephant.
8. In what year was the Prophet Muhammad born?
9. Relate the important events that took place in the Prophet's life between his birth and thirty-five years of age.
10. Why did people always believe that the Prophet possessed exceptional qualities?

After Prophethood

1. What events surrounded the first revelation of the Holy Qur'an?
2. Write down the names of the first Muslims.
3. Give three quotations from the Holy Qur'an in which the Prophet is commanded to proclaim the faith of Allah.
4. Why were the Quraysh frightened of Islam?
5. Describe the persecution inflicted by the Quraysh on (a) 'Ammar, (b) Bilal, (c) Mus'ab ibn 'Umayr and (d) Abu Bakr.

6. Describe how the Quraysh persecuted the Prophet.
7. In your own words describe what happened when 'Utbah, on behalf of the Quraysh, went to negotiate with the Prophet.
8. Describe the *hijrah* to Abyssinia and the failure of the Qurayshi mission.
9. Describe the events surrounding the acceptance of Islam by 'Umar ibn al-Khattab.
10. Describe the boycott and the harsh conditions to which the Muslims were subjected in the *She'b Abi Talib*.
11. What sad events met the Prophet when he went to Ta'if?
12. Explain the meaning in the Holy Qur'an of 53: 17, 18.
13. What events led up to the *hijrah* to Madinah?
14. Describe the Prophet's journey to Madinah.
15. Explain the meaning in the Holy Qur'an of 40: 9.

In Madinah

1. Describe the scene in Madinah as the people awaited the Prophet's arrival.
2. Make a list of the Prophet's exemplary actions when he arrived in Madinah.
3. How did the *adhan* originate?
4. Explain the meaning in the Holy Qur'an of 2: 143.

5. When was fasting made obligatory?

The Decisive Battle of Badr

1. Why was it necessary for the Prophet to seek certain reassurances from the Ansar before he could confront the Quraysh?
2. How many Muslims set out to fight and how many men had the Quraysh mustered?
3. Explain the meaning in the Holy Qur'an of 8: 11.
4. Bearing in mind what the Holy Qur'an says in 3: 123, explain how the small band of Muslims managed to defeat the Quraysh.
5. What did the Prophet do with his Quraysh captives?

The Battle of Uhud

1. Why did the Quraysh want to start another war against the Muslims?
2. How many Muslims accompanied the Prophet when he left to fight outside Madinah?
3. Why did one-third of the Prophet's Companions withdraw from fighting?
4. In what ways were the Muslims severely tested during this battle?
5. The Muslim archers did not follow the Prophet's order to remain in their positions. What was the result of their disobedience?

6. What injuries did the Prophet suffer during this battle?
7. How many Muslims were martyred during this battle? Name the leading Companions who were martyred.
8. Why did the Muslims decide to continue to pursue the Quraysh army?

The Battle of the Ditch

1. Why were the Quraysh and the Jews eager to forge an alliance against the Muslims?
2. How large was the total enemy army?
3. How many Muslims defended Madinah?
4. What did Salman al-Farsi suggest that the Muslims do to protect themselves from attack?
5. Describe some of the miracles the Companions witnessed at this time.
6. What happened when the first Qurayshi horseman jumped the ditch?
7. How long did the siege last?
8. In your own words, write the story of how Nu'aym ibn Mas'ud split the alliance between the Quraysh and the Ghatafan.
9. Explain the meaning in the Holy Qur'an of 33: 9.
10. Did the Quraysh ever again go to Madinah to attack the Muslims?

The Expedition Against the Banu Qurayzah

1. What obligations and clauses were contained in the covenant drawn up between the Muhajirun and the Ansar to which the Jews were also a party?
2. Write down the verse in the Holy Qur'an which refers to the hostility against Islam when the treaty was broken.
3. For how many days did the Muslims lay siege to the Banu Qurayzah?
4. What was the judgement of Sa'd ibn Mu'adh that conformed with the law of war laid down in the Torah?
5. What important measure did Thumamah take against the Quraysh when he became a Muslim?

The Peace Treaty of Hudaybiyyah

1. In which year did the Prophet leave Madinah to perform 'Umrah?
2. How many Muslims accompanied the Prophet on his journey?
3. How did the Quraysh react to the Muslims' arrival at Hudaybiyyah?
4. Explain the meaning in the Holy Qur'an of 48: 18.
5. What happened when the Quraysh sent Suhayl ibn 'Amr to the Prophet?
6. What conditions were contained in the Treaty of Hudaybiyyah?

7. What action of the Prophet's raised the spirits of the Muslims before they left Hudaybiyyah?
8. Explain the meaning in the Holy Qur'an of 48: 1–3.
9. What benefits did the Treaty of Hudaybiyyah bring to the Muslims?
10. Explain the meaning in the Holy Qur'an of 2: 216.

Inviting the Kings and Rulers to Islam

1. List the foreign rulers to whom the Prophet sent letters inviting them to accept Islam.
2. What did Heraclius do after receiving his letter?
3. How did the King of Abyssinia and the King of Egypt react to the letters they received?
4. What was the immediate reaction of the emperor of Persia to the letter he received?
5. What did the Prophet foretell would happen to the Persian empire?

The Expedition to Khaybar

1. Why did the Prophet want to subdue the Jewish colony at Khaybar?
2. How many Muslims set off for Khaybar?
3. How many women accompanied this expedition, and for what purpose?
4. List five important events that took place during the Battle of Khaybar.

5. What were the conditions contained in the peace treaty?
6. During this expedition an attempt was made to poison the Prophet. Describe the way in which the poison was administered.
7. Give the reason why the Jewess who administered the poison was punished later.
8. What did the Quraysh do when the Muslims went to Makkah for *'umrah* in 7 A.H?
9. The attitude towards baby girls changed after the advent of Islam. Describe the changed attitudes.
10. To what does the term *mawla* refer?

The Expedition to Mu'tah

1. Why was it necessary for the lives of the Prophet's envoys to be protected?
2. Which Muslim envoy was killed by Shurahbil ibn 'Amr al-Ghassani, the provincial governor of Busra under the Byzantine emperor Heraclius?
3. How many Muslims were in the military force that set out for Busra and how many Romans and Arabs were in Heraclius' army?
4. On what grounds did the Muslims go ahead to fight the massive enemy force?
5. How did the battle end and what effect did it have on the Muslims in Madinah? What was the Prophet's comment on the civilians' attitude towards the army?

The Conquest of Makkah

1. Describe how the Peace Treaty of Hudaybiyyah was broken.
2. What happened when Abu Sufyan came into the home of his daughter, Umm Habibah, who was married to the Prophet?
3. How many believers accompanied the Prophet when he went to Makkah in Ramadan 8 A.H.?
4. Under what circumstances did Abu Sufyan accept Islam?
5. How did the Prophet ensure that the Makkans would not be killed unnecessarily when the Muslims entered Makkah?
6. What scene did the Prophet show to Abu Sufyan? What effect did it have on him?
7. What significant event took place on 20 Ramadan 8 A.H.?
8. Explain the meaning in the Holy Qur'an of 17: 81 and 34: 49.
9. What did the Prophet say when he entered the Ka'bah with the Muslims for the first time?
10. List the important events that took place while the Prophet was in Makkah at this time.

The Battle of Hunayn

1. Once the Quraysh had submitted to Islam, which other powerful tribe called for war against the Muslims?

2. How many Muslims from Makkah and how many from Madinah set out to confront the enemy at Hunayn?

3. How did the Hawazin terrify the Muslims when they arrived at Hunayn?

4. Why did Allah choose to chastise the Muslims?

5. Explain the meaning in the Holy Qur'an of 9: 25, 26.

The Expedition of Ta'if

1. Which tribe had supported the Hawazin and then retreated to Ta'if to prepare for another war against the Muslims?

2. For how many days did the Muslims lay siege to Ta'if?

3. Why was the Prophet prepared to leave Ta'if without conquering it?

4. Why did the Prophet stop at al-Ji'irranah for about two weeks on his way back from Ta'if?

5. What happened when a delegation from the Thaqif came to the Prophet and accepted Islam?

The Tabuk Expedition

1. Why was it necessary to make the Tabuk expedition?

2. How many Muslims accompanied the Prophet to Tabuk?

3. Why did the Romans decide not to invade the Muslim lands?
4. After Tabuk the Muslims could live in peace. Show how that security had a beneficial effect for Muslim women.
5. When was the first *Hajj* made obligatory? How many Muslims left Madinah for that first *Hajj* and who was their amir?

The Year of Delegations

1. Imagine yourself as an Arab visitor to Madinah in 10 A.H. Write a short report describing your first encounters with Muslims.
2. What message did the Prophet send to Yemen?
3. Which tribe did Dimam ibn Tha'labah represent when he visited Madinah and what was he determined to do when he returned to his people?
4. In which year was *Zakat* made compulsory?
5. What encouraged 'Adi ibn Hatim to become a Muslim and what comment did he make?

The Farewell *Hajj*

1. List five reasons why Allah allowed the Prophet to perform the Farewell *Hajj*.
2. What was the Prophet's first action when he entered Makkah?
3. List the main points in the Prophet's *Khutbah*, delivered from the back of his camel.

4. What did the Muslims reply in unison when the Prophet finished his sermon?

5. List the important events that took place during the Farewell *Hajj*.

The Death of the Messenger of Allah

1. Explain the meaning in the Holy Qur'an of 5: 3.
2. Who led the Muslims in prayer while the Prophet was ill?
3. What warning did the Prophet give to Muslims relating to the graves of earlier Prophets?
4. What were the Prophet's last words?
5. What was the date of the Prophet's death and what was his age at that time?

The Prophet's Character and Qualities

1. Describe the Prophet's exemplary character according to the words of 'Ali ibn Abi Talib.
2. List some of the chores the Prophet always insisted on doing for himself.
3. Describe the behaviour of the Prophet when he was among other people.
4. Describe the Prophet's appearance according to the words of Abu Hurayrah.
5. Describe the Prophet according to the words of Anas.

TRANSLITERATION

Consonants. Arabic

initial: unexpressed
medial and final:

ء	ʾ	د	d	ض	ḍ	ك k
ب	b	ذ	dh	ط	ṭ	ل l
ت	t	ر	r	ظ	ẓ	م m
ث	th	ز	z	ع	ʿ	ن n
ج	j	س	s	غ	gh	ه h
ح	ḥ	ش	sh	ف	f	و w
خ	kh	ص	ṣ	ق	q	ي y

Vowels, diphthongs, etc.

short: َ a; ِ i; ُ u.

long: ‎ـَا ā ‎ـُو ū ‎ـِي ī ‎ىّ īy

diphthongs: ‎ـَوْ aw

‎ـَىْ ay

Glossary

Adhān: Call to prayers.

Anṣār: Helpers; title of the people of Madīnah who helped the Prophet and his Companions when they migrated from Makkah to Madīnah.

'Aṣr: Late afternoon prayer.

Ayyām at-Tashrīq: The three days (11th, 12th, 13th) of the twelfth month of the Islamic calendar.

Bay'at-ar-Riḍwān, the Pledge of the Pleasure. The Pledge which took place at al-Hudaybiyyah and upon which Allah the Almighty revealed a special verse of the Qur'ān to express His Pleasure with those believers who gave their allegiance to the Prophet.

Dhu'l-Ḥijjah: The month of Ḥajj, twelfth month of the Islamic calendar.

Dhu'l-Qa'dah: The eleventh month of the Islamic calendar.

Fajr: Morning prayer, which is offered after dawn and before sunrise.

Fijār: Sacrilegious war. This battle took place among the Arabs before Islam. It was given this name because it violated the sacredness of the *ḥaram* and the sacred months. These months were regarded as sacred and respected among the Arabs even before Islam.

Ghazwah Dhāt ar-Riqā': The battle of the rugs. This name was given to this battle because the people who took part were bare footed and the land was rough so, when their feet became blistered, they bandaged them with torn-up strips of clothing.

Ḥajj: The Pilgrimage.

Ḥajjat al-Balāgh: The Pilgrimage of conveying the message.

Ḥajjat al-Wadā': The Farewell Pilgrimage – when the Prophet bade farewell to his *Ummah*.

Ḥanīfiyyah: To devote oneself fully to Allah and completely surrender to His will. This is the name of the religion of Prophet Ibrāhīm (peace and blessings be upon him).

Ḥijr: Known as *Ḥaṭīm*, it is the half-walled area attached to the Ka'bah which is also called *Ḥijr-Ismā'īl* and *Ḥijr al-Ka'bah*.

Hijrah: Migration in the way of Allah.

Ḥilf al-Fuḍūl (the alliance of excellence): This alliance was called *ḥilf al-Fuḍūl*, due to the excellence of the contents of this agreement.

Hubal: One of the major idols in pre-Islamic Arabia.

Imām: The person who leads the prayer; also refers to the leader of Muslims.

Iqāmah: The final call to prayer which is given just before the start of the prayer.

'Ishā': The night prayer.

Jāhiliyyah: The age of Ignorance. This name was given to the period between Prophet 'Īsā and the Prophet Muḥammad when people forgot the teachings of the Prophets, and violated the religious sanctities.

Jamrat al-'Aqabah: The symbol of the ritual of stoning Shayṭān in Minā which is located near 'Aqabah.

Jamrat al-'Ūlā: The first symbol of the ritual of stoning Shayṭān in Minā.

Jamrat al-Wusṭā: The second (medium) symbol of stoning Shayṭān.

Jihād: To struggle or fight in the way of Allah.

Jinn: They are created by Allah from fire, and are invisible to human beings. They can change their shape. They are also subject to the Islamic call. Among them there are believers and unbelievers.

Jizyah: The tax which is levied in Muslim states on non-Muslim adult subjects who can afford it in return for security for their lives and property and defending them against their enemies.

Jumāda'l-'Ūlā: The fifth month of the Islamic calendar.

Jumu'ah: The Friday prayer.

Kāfir: The unbeliever who rejects Islam or violates its basic beliefs.

Khiṭbah: Marriage proposal.

Khuṭbah: The sermon.

Kunyah: A type of surname or proper name common in Arabic which means father of so and so or mother of so and so. It is regarded as a mark of honour for a person.

Lāt: One of the major idols in pre-Islamic Arabia.

Madrasah: School; generally refers to the Islamic school.

Maghrib: The prayer which is performed just after sunset.

Manāt: One of the major idols in pre-Islamic Arabia.

Mawlā: Refers to master, lord, guardian, protector and friend. This term also applies to a freed slave and to the person who frees the slave.

Minbar: Pulpit.

Miswāk: Tooth stick.

Mu'adhdhin: The caller of *Adhān*, inviting Muslims to prayer.

al-Mu'awwidhatayn: The last two *sūrahs* of the Qur'ān, i.e. *Sūrah al-Falaq* and *Sūrah an-Nās*.

Muhājir: Emigrant; a person who migrates in the way of Allah.

Muhājirūn: Emigrants; title given to Muslims who migrated from Makkah to Madīnah.

Qiblah: The direction which Muslims face in prayer.

al-Qullays: The church which Abrahah built in San'ā, intending to divert Arabs from the Ka'bah in Makkah to it.

Rabī' al-Awwal: The third month of the Islamic calendar.

Rak'at: One unit of a prayer.

Ramaḍān: The ninth month of the Islamic calendar.

Rukū': Ritual of bowing down in prayer.

Ṣadaqah: Charity in the way of Allah.

Ṣafar: The second month of the Islamic calendar.

Sajdah: Prostration in the prayer.

Ṣalātu'l-Fatḥ: The prayer of thanksgiving to Allah at a time of victory.

Ṣā': A cubic measurement of grain which weighs around 3.2kg.

Shawwāl: The tenth month of the Islamic calendar.

Sa'y: Ritual of running between Ṣafā and Marwah in Ḥajj and 'Umrah.

She'b Abī Ṭālib: Abū Ṭālib's quarters – an area in Makkah in which the Banū Hāshim were abandoned when the Quraysh unbelievers boycotted them.

Shirk: Associating other things with Allah.

aṣ-Ṣiḥāḥ: The authentic books of Ḥadīth.

Sīrah: The life of the Prophet Muḥammad.

Sunan: Plural of *Sunnah,* the way of the Prophet; implies here the supererogatory works of Ḥajj and general way and manners of Prophets performing the Ḥajj.

Sūrah: A chapter of the Qur'ān.

Sūrat al-Fatḥ: The chapter of victory (Chapter 48).

Taqwā: Piety – fear of Allah/consciousness in religion.

Tarwiyah: The eighth day of the twelfth month of the Islamic calendar.

Ṭawāf: Circling the Ka'bah in worship.

Ṭawāf al-Ifāḍah/Ṭawāf az-Ziārah: The obligatory *Ṭawāf* of *Ḥajj.*

Tawḥīd: Oneness of God.

Ummah: Nation, community – terms used for the community who accepted the Prophet's message.

Umm al-Mu'minīn: The mothers of the believers – title given to the wives of the Prophet Muḥammad (peace be upon him) because they are regarded as the mothers of all believers.

'Umrah: The lesser Pilgrimage.

'Umrat al-Qaḍā': The fulfilled *'Umrah* – the *'Umrah* which the Prophet performed in the seventh year after *Hijrah* which he intended to do in the sixth year but the Quraysh unbelievers had not allowed him to complete.

'Uzzā: One of the major idols in pre-Islamic Arabia.

Ẓuhr: The afternoon prayer.

Names/Kunyahs/Epithets and Titles

al-'Abbās ibn 'Abdu'l-Muṭṭalib (Abu'l-Faḍl)
'Abd Manāf
'Abdullāh (aṭ-Ṭāhir, aṭ-Ṭayyib)
'Abdullāh ibn Abī Rabī'ah
'Abdullāh ibn Jaḥsh
'Abdullāh ibn Jubayr
'Abdullāh ibn Jud'ān
'Abdullāh ibn Mas'ūd
'Abdullāh ibn Rawāḥah
'Abdullāh ibn Salām
'Abdullāh ibn Ubayy ibn Salūl
'Abdullāh ibn Urayqiṭ
'Abdu'l-Muṭṭalib
'Abdu'r-Raḥmān ibn Abī Bakr
'Abdu'r-Raḥmān ibn 'Awf
Abrahah al-Ashram
Abū Ayyūb Khālid ibn Zayd al-Anṣāri
Abū Bakr ibn Abī Quḥāfah
Abū Baṣīr 'Utbah ibn Usayd
Abū Dujānah
Abū Hālah
Abū Ḥudhayfah
Abū Hurayrah
Abū Jandal ibn Suhayl
Abū Lahab
Abu'l-Ḥakam ibn Hishām (Abū Jahl)
Abū Ma'bad
Abū Mūsā
Abū Sa'īd al-Khudrī
Abū Salamah
Abū Sufyān ibn Ḥarb
Abū Sufyan ibn al-Ḥārith ibn 'Abdu'l-Muṭṭalib
Abū Ṭalḥah al-Anṣārī
Abū Ṭalib
Abū 'Ubaydah ibn al-Jarrāḥ
Ādam

'Addās
'Adī
'Adnān
'Ā'ishah aṣ-Ṣiddīqah bint Abī Bakr aṣ-Ṣiddīq
'Ali ibn Abī Ṭālib
Āminah
'Āmir ibn al-Akwa'
'Āmir ibn Fuhayrah
'Āmir ibn Mālik
'Ammār ibn Yāsir
'Amr ibn 'Abd Wudd
'Amr ibn al-'Āṣ ibn Wā'il
'Amr ibn al-Jamūḥ
'Amr ibn Luḥayy
'Amr ibn Sālim al-Khuzā'ī
Anas ibn Mālik al-Anṣāri
Anas ibn an-Naḍr
'Aqīl
al-Arqam ibn Abi'l-Arqam
As'ad ibn Zurārah
al-'Āṣ ibn Wā'il
'Aṣim ibn Thābit
Asmā' bint Abī Bakr
'Ātikah bint 'Abdu'l-Muṭṭalib

Bābawayh
Bādhān
al-Barā' ibn 'Āzib
Bilāl ibn Rabāḥ al-Ḥabashī
Bishr ibn al-Barā' ibn Ma'rūr

Ḍimām ibn Tha'labah

Faḍl ibn 'Abbās
Fatimah
Faṭimah bint al-Khaṭṭāb
Fihr ibn Mālik

Ghālib

Ḥafṣah bint 'Umar ibn al-Khaṭṭāb
Hājar
Ḥalīmah as-Sa'diyah
Hamzah ibn 'Abdu'l-Muṭṭalib
Ḥarām ibn Milḥān
al-Ḥārith ibn 'Umayr al-Azdī
Ḥasan
Hāshim
Ḥātim
Hilāl ibn Umayyah
Hind bint Abī Umayyah al-Qurashiyyah al-Makhzūmiyyah
Hind bint 'Utbah
Hishām ibn 'Amr ibn Rabī'ah
Ḥudhayfah ibn al-Yamān
Ḥusayn
Ḥuyayy ibn Akhṭab

Ibn Hishām
Ibrāhīm
'Ikrimah ibn Abī Jahl
Ilyās
'Īsā ibn Maryam
Ismā'īl

Jabbār ibn Sulmā
Ja'far ibn Abī Ṭālib (aṭ-Ṭayyār, Dhu'l-Janāḥayn)
Jibrīl
Jubayr ibn Muṭ'im
Juwayriyyah bint al-Ḥārith ibn Abī Ḍirār al-Muṣṭaliqiyyah

Ka'b
Ka'b ibn Asad al-Quraẓī
Ka'b ibn Mālik
Ka'b ibn Zayd
Khabbāb ibn al-Aratt
Khadījah bint Khuwaylid al-Qurashiyyah al-Asadiyyah
Khālid ibn al-Walīd
Khubayb ibn 'Adī
Khuzaymah
Kilāb
Kinānah

Lu'ayy

Ma'add
Maḥmūd
Mālik
Mālik ibn 'Awf an-Naṣri
Mālik ibn Sinān
Marḥab
Māriyah bint Sham'ūn
Maymūnah bint al-Ḥārith al-Hilāliyyah
al-Miqdād
Mu'ādh ibn Jabal
Muḍar
Mudrikah
Muḥammad ibn 'Abdullāh ibn 'Abdu'l-Muṭṭalib ibn Hāshim ibn 'Abd Manāf ibn Quṣayy ibn Kilāb ibn Murrah ibn Ka'b ibn Lu'ayy ibn Ghālib ibn Fihr ibn Mālik ibn an-Naḍr ibn Kinānah ibn Khuzaymah ibn Mudrikah ibn Ilyās ibn Muḍar ibn Nizār ibn Ma'add ibn 'Adnān
Murārah ibn ar-Rabī'
Murrah
Mūsā
Muṣ'ab ibn 'Umayr
al-Muṭ'im ibn 'Adī

an-Naḍr
Nā'im
Nizār
Nu'aym ibn 'Abdullāh
Nu'aym ibn Mas'ūd

al-Qāsim
Qatādah ibn an-Nu'mān
Quṣayy ibn Kilāb

Rāfi' ibn Khadīj
Rayḥānah bint Zayd
Ruqayyah

Sa'd ibn Abī Waqqāṣ
Sa'd ibn Mu'ādh (Abū 'Amr)
Sa'd ibn ar-Rabī'
Sa'd ibn 'Ubādah
Ṣafiyyah bint 'Abdu'l-Muṭṭalib
Ṣafiyyah bint Ḥuyayy ibn Akhṭab
Ṣafwān ibn Umayyah

Sa'īd ibn Zayd
Sallām ibn Abi'l-Huqayq
Sallām ibn Mishkam
Salmān al-Fārsī
Samurah ibn Jundub
Sawdah bint Zam'ah al-Qurashiyyah
as-Sīrah an-Nabawiyyah (Book)
Shaybah ibn Rabī'ah
ash-Shaymā' bint Halīmah as-Sa'diyah
Sherawayh
Shu'ayb
Shurahbīl ibn 'Amr al-Ghassānī
Suhayb
Suhayl ibn 'Amr
 Surāqah ibn Mālik ibn Ju'sham

Talhah ibn 'Ubaydullāh
Thumāmah ibn Uthāl
at-Tufayl ibn 'Amr ad-Dawsi

'Ubaydah ibn al-Hārith ibn al-Muttalib ibn 'Abd Manāf
Ubayy ibn Khalaf
Umāmah
'Umar ibn al-Khattāb
Umaymah
Umm Ayman
Umm Habībah bint Abī Sufyān
Umm Hānī bint Abī Tālib
Umm Jamīl
Umm Khayr
Umm Kulthūm
Umm Ma'bad al-Khuzā'iyyah
Umm Salamah
Umm Sulaym
Umm Sulayt
'Umayr ibn Abī Waqqas
'Umayr ibn al-Humām al-Ansārī
Umayyah ibn Khalaf
'Uqbah ibn Abī Mu'ayt
'Urwah ibn Mas'ūd ath-Thaqafī
Usamāh ibn Zayd ibn Hārithah
Usayd ibn Hudayr
'Utbah ibn Rabī'ah (Abu'l Walīd)
'Uthmān ibn 'Affān
'Uthmān ibn Maz'ūn
'Uthmān ibn Talhah

Wahb
Wahshī
al-Walīd ibn al-Mughīrah (Abū 'Abd Shams)
al-Walīd ibn 'Utbah
Waraqah ibn Nawfal

Zayd ibn ad' Dathinah
Zayd ibn Hārithah
Zayd ibn Thābit
Zaynab
Zaynab bint al-Hārith
Zaynab bint Jahsh
Zaynab bint Khuzaymah
Ziyād ibn as-Sakan
az-Zubayr ibn al-'Awwām
Zuhayr ibn Abī Umayyah

Communities, Tribes, Clans and Families

'Adal
Aws

Banū 'Abd Manāf
Banū 'Abdu'd-Dār
Banū Abdu'l-Ashhal
Banū 'Abdu'l-Muttalib
Banū 'Adī
Banū 'Āmir
Banū Bakr
Banū Dīnār
Banū Fazārah
Banū Fihr
Banū Hanīfah
Banū Hārithah
Banū Hāshim
Banū Ka'b
Banū Khuzā'ah
Banū Makhzūm
Banū Mālik ibn an-Najjār
Banū al-Muttalib
Banu'n-Nadīr
Banū Qaynuqā'
Banū Qurayzah
Banū Sa'd ibn Bakr

Banū Sā'idah
Banū Sālim ibn 'Awf
Banū Sulaym
Banū Tamīm
Banū Taym
Banū Wā'il
Banū Zuhrah

Dhakwān

Ghatafān

Hawāzin

Khazraj
Kinānah

al-Qārah
Quraysh

Ri'l

Thamūd
Thaqīf

'Usayyah

Places

al-Abwā'
'Aqabah
'Arafāt

Badr
al-Balqā'
al-Baqī'
Bark Ghamdān
Buṣrā

Dār an-Nadwah
ad-Dārūn
Dhu'l-Ḥulayfah

Fadak

Ghazzah

Ḥamrā' al-Asad
Ḥaram
al-Ḥijr
Ḥijr
Ḥirah
Ḥudaybiyyah
Ḥunayn

al-Jurf

Ka'bah
Khaybar

Ma'ān
al-Madā'in
Madīnah

Makkah
Marr aẓ-Ẓahrān
Marwah
al-Mash'ar al-Ḥarām
al-Masjid al-Aqṣā
al-Masjid al-Ḥarām
Minā
Mu'tah
Muzdalifah

Nakhl

Qubā'

Ṣafā
Ṣan'ā'
ash-Shawṭ
She'b Abī Ṭālib

Tabūk
Ṭā'if
Taymā'
Thaniyyat al-Wadā'
Thawr

Uḥud
'Usfān

Wādi'l-Qurā

Yamāmah
Yathrib

Zabīd
Zamzam